I0795221

Morning Comes to Elk Mountain

Dispatches from the
Wichita Mountains Wildlife Refuge

Morning Comes to Elk Mountain

Dispatches from the Wichita Mountains Wildlife Refuge

Gary Lantz

foreword by David Taylor

Number 1 in the Southwestern Nature Writing Series

UNIVERSITY OF NORTH TEXAS PRESS
DENTON, TEXAS

Printed in the United States of America.

10 9 8 7 6 5 4 3 2 1

Permissions:
University of North Texas Press
1155 Union Circle #311336
Denton, TX 76203-5017

The paper used in this book meets the minimum requirements of the American National Standard for Permanence of Paper for Printed Library Materials, z39.48.1984. Binding materials have been chosen for durability.

Library of Congress Cataloging-in-Publication Data
Lantz, Gary, 1947-
Morning comes to Elk Mountain : dispatches from the Wichita Mountains Wildlife Refuge / by Gary Lantz ; foreword by David Taylor. -- 1st ed.
p. cm. -- (Number 1 in the Southwestern nature writing series)
Includes index.
ISBN 978-1-57441-527-8 (cloth : alk. paper) -- ISBN 978-1-57441-539-1 (pbk. : alk. paper) -- ISBN 978-1-57441-536-0 (ebook)
1. Wichita Mountains Wildlife Refuge (Okla.) 2. Natural history--Oklahoma--Wichita Mountains. 3. Wildlife conservation--Oklahoma--Wichita Mountains. 4. Wichita Mountains (Okla.) I. Title. II. Series: Southwestern nature writing series ; no. 1.
QL84.22.O5L36 2013
333.95'41609766--dc23
2013018244

Morning Comes to Elk Mountain: Dispatches from the Wichita Mountains National Wildlife Refuge is Number 1 in the Southwestern Nature Writing Series

The electronic edition of this book was made possible by the support of the Vick Family Foundation.

Contents

Color photos follow page 116.

Foreword by David Taylor

In June 2012, I had the good fortune to meet Gary Lantz at the Wichita Mountains Wildlife Refuge. When driving up from Dallas by way of Wichita Falls, the mountains slowly overwhelm the northwest horizon. In an area defined by flatness, these granite projections are the focal point going north on Hwy. 46 from Texas. It was a relatively mild, early summer day and though we'd been in a long-term drought, we had had some rain the last few weeks. The refuge was a mix of pink, rounded, granite boulders and knobs jutting up from green pastures with stipple brush dots of yellow, red, blue and pink wildflowers. Not far from the Visitors Center a few bison grazed, like huge black boulders slowly rolling across the fields. Gary was to be my guide for the day. I had read much of his writing about the Wichita Mountains, but he wanted to introduce me directly to this place, and I wanted to spend some time with an excellent naturalist in a place that he loved. What struck me that day are two things: one, what a dramatic landscape the Wichita Mountains are, and two, what a close relationship Gary has built with them.

The Wichita Mountains Wildlife Refuge has a remarkable history. It is difficult to express just how unique, if not shocking, it is to see these mountains projecting up out of the plains. As Gary notes,

Native Americans considered them sacred ground, explorers and pioneers liked to imagine the possibility of gold, Teddy Roosevelt saw in them a remnant landscape of the old west, and nowadays they are the alien landscape getaway from surrounding tabletop/flatland geography. Bison roam somewhat freely, prairie dog towns pop up in places along the road, and somewhere up in the mountains, introduced Rocky Mountain elk make their way among the boulders. The surrounding settlement of Medicine Creek too has a kind of foreign flair to it given its past as an early 20th-century vacation retreat. I was struck by just how exotic it all felt to me, even though I was born less than 100 miles away as the crow flies. Maybe another way of saying this is that in order to get closer to understanding the Wichita Mountains, it helps to have a guide walk with you from the surrounding plains into this place.

Walking with Gary Lantz isn't really walking, it's being taught to see. You could go no more than ten to fifteen feet down the trail and spend most of the day. Gary will show you the less obvious flowers you didn't know; point to the grasses and forbs you didn't see; identify animal signs you ignored; and describe the ecological relationship behind the scientific and common names for all that he's just offered. After that he can tell you about the human history of some of the invasive species or the preservation efforts over the last hundred years to save some of the native ones. Gary can also add personal stories about his own forty-year relationship with the Wichita Mountains, but he'll give you all of the above before offering the latter. Gary has about him a kindness and patience in his voice (he endured my endless, goofy questions about this flower, that geology, Fort Sill, and the nearby town of Medicine Creek). His writing style reminds me of the best in American natural history writing: solid, engaging naturalist description offered with a narrative voice of patience and curiosity. Such writers will use narrative, but they are thoughtful enough to put their own story after what's actually in front of them. In other words, there's a maturity to his person that emanates in his writing. Gary is also a superb photographer. All the time he's offering you these details and stories, he's focusing and refocusing his camera, taking pictures—close-ups, landscapes and panoramas. It's as though he finds combining the pictures he's taking with his naturalist's knowledge and his personal stories might begin to offer walking companions and readers a bit of the view he has.

My day with Gary Lantz in the Wichita Mountains Wildlife Refuge is one of my prized outdoor experiences. I was in a marvelous place and was offered a view of it by someone who knows it well. The book before you will offer the same feeling I had that day—the joy of having a knowledgeable guide take you to a place he loves. The chapters follow from month to month in a calendar year; each offers a new perspective based on seasonal changes and the stories that connect to what's there at that time. These descriptions, photographs, histories and stories build upon the previous ones to tell a bigger story, one which Gary has spent forty years preparing to tell. Read and listen; you will be rewarded.

David Taylor, editor,
University of North Texas Southwestern Nature Writing Series

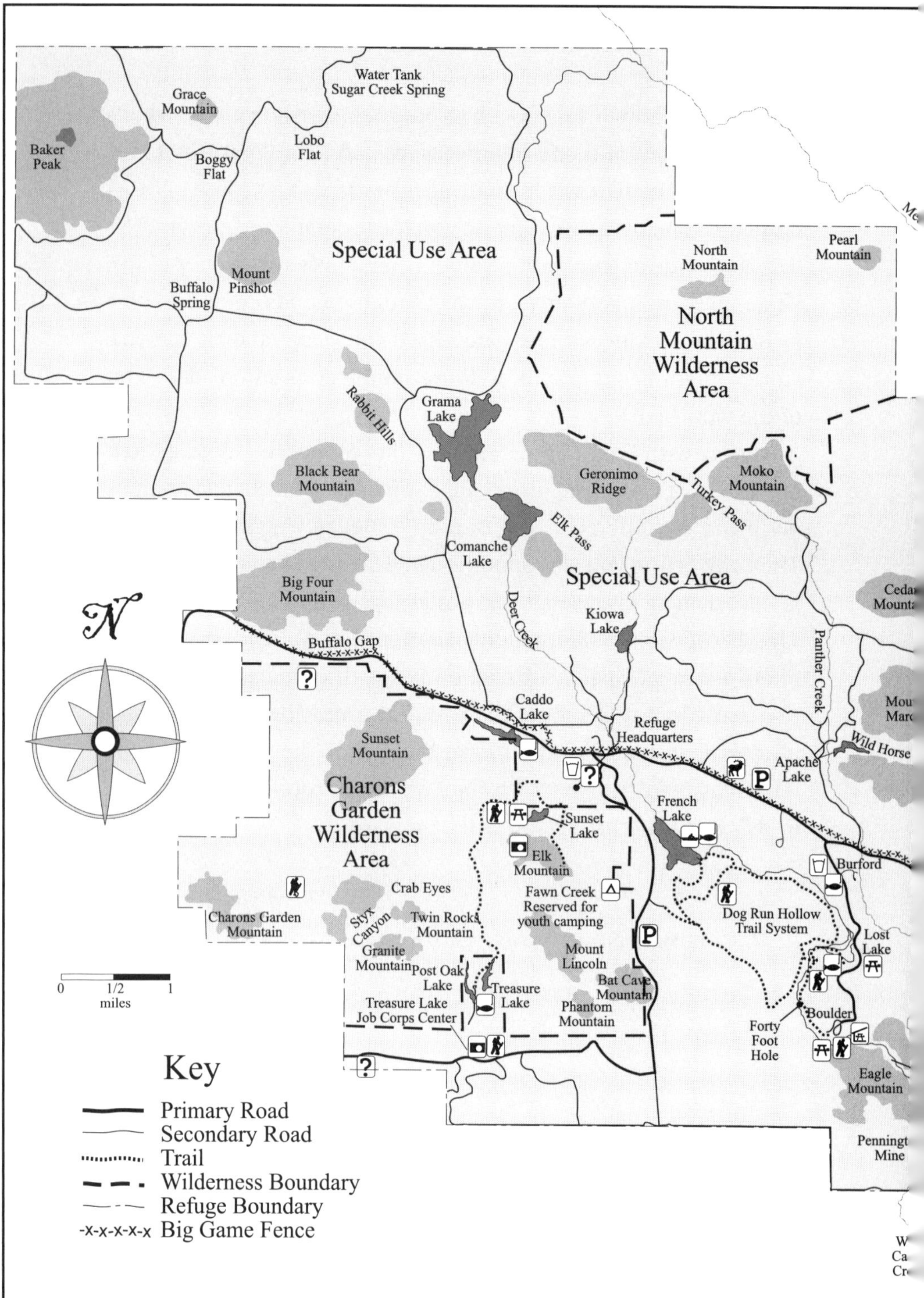

Water Tank
Sugar Creek Spring
Grace Mountain
Baker Peak
Lobo Flat
Boggy Flat
Special Use Area
North Mountain
Pearl Mountain
Mount Pinshot
Buffalo Spring
North Mountain Wilderness Area
Rabbit Hills
Grama Lake
Black Bear Mountain
Geronimo Ridge
Moko Mountain
Turkey Pass
Elk Pass
Comanche Lake
Big Four Mountain
Deer Creek
Special Use Area
Kiowa Lake
Panther Creek
Buffalo Gap
Caddo Lake
Refuge Headquarters
Sunset Mountain
Wild Horse
Apache Lake
Charons Garden Wilderness Area
French Lake
Sunset Lake
Elk Mountain
Burford
Crab Eyes
Fawn Creek Reserved for youth camping
Dog Run Hollow Trail System
Charons Garden Mountain
Styx Canyon
Twin Rocks Mountain
Granite Mountain
Mount Lincoln
Lost Lake
Post Oak Lake
Treasure Lake
Bat Cave Mountain
Treasure Lake Job Corps Center
Phantom Mountain
Boulder
Forty Foot Hole
Eagle Mountain
0 1/2 1
miles
Key
Primary Road
Secondary Road
Trail
Wilderness Boundary
Refuge Boundary
-x-x-x-x-x Big Game Fence

Wichita Mountains Wildlife Refuge

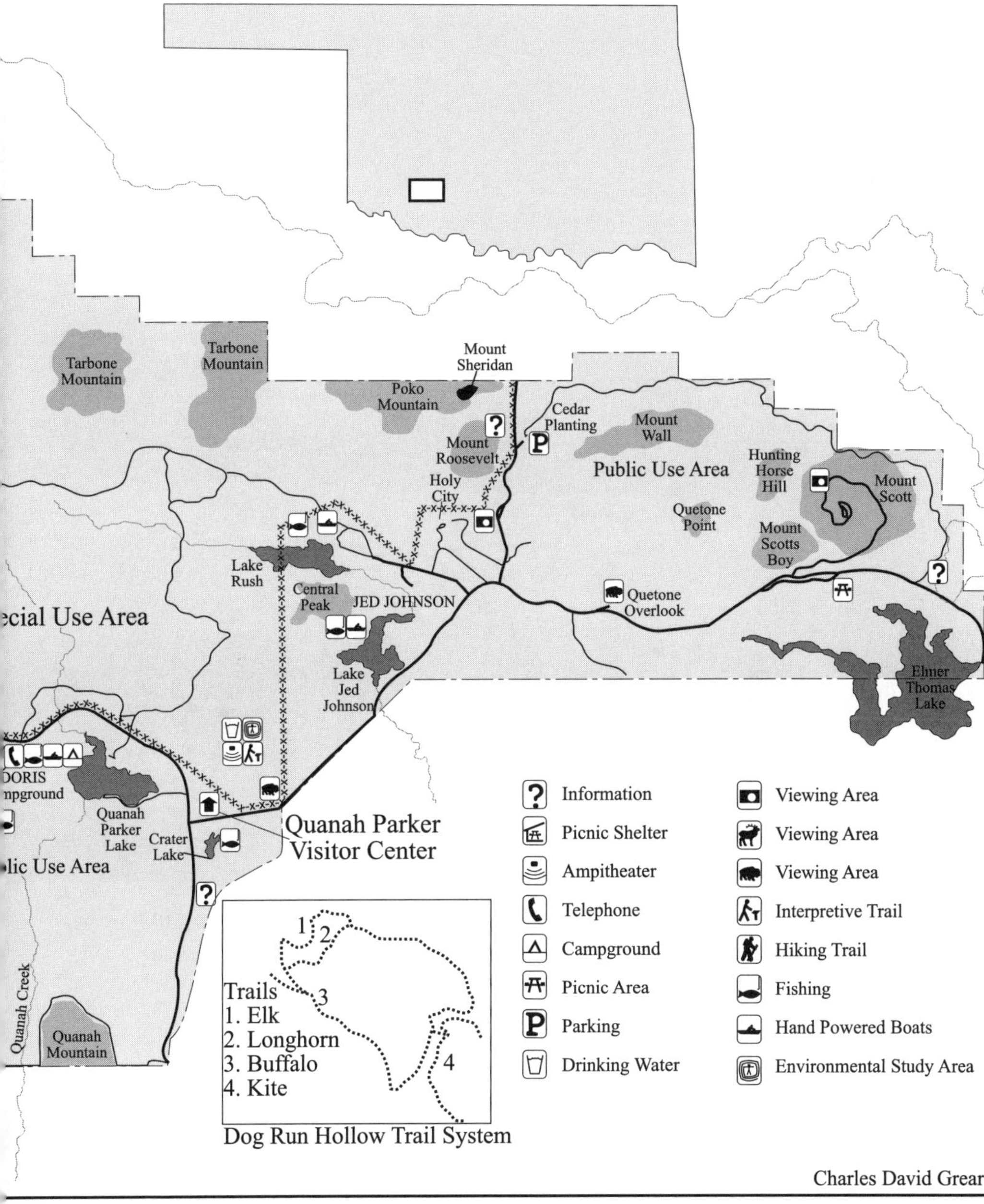

ANCIENT ROCK. A sweeping view of the Wichita Mountains Wildlife Refuge from atop Mount Scott, second highest point in the Wichitas.

Introduction

The Wichita Mountains are an oddity in a region better known for barrenness. You'll never run across a ski lift here, nor very much snow, for that matter. The weather is fickle to the point of being problematic. Numbing blizzards interrupt mild winters. Weeks of spring-like weather can be punctuated by ice storms that shear off tree limbs. Droughts that drag on for what seems an eternity are broken by storms that dump several inches of water in a matter of minutes—and then may be followed by a tornado with enough wind speed and rotating volatility to fling automobiles into the air.

Some say the weather on the Southern Plains is the harshest in the world. And they generally say it from somewhere else, having fled a beating at the hands of brutal sun, wind, ice, and fickle rainfall. However, the weather here is generally good enough, if and when the rains arrive on a reasonable basis, to grow a decent mouthful of grass. Before the white man arrived, this grass, coupled with fresh water flowing from springs scattered throughout the rock, attracted the American buffalo of western folklore, or bison of modern scientific nomenclature, by the millions. Along with the buffalo were deer, elk, pronghorn antelope, and black bear. Following close behind all this flesh on the hoof were packs of wolves.

The earliest Anglo visitors to the region gushed over the abundant wildlife. They also marveled at the size of the Indian villages bordering the mountains, a landscape where the tribes—Kiowa, Comanche, and Wichita in particular—could find potable water, wood for cooking and warmth, protein on the hoof for hunting and ample grass for grazing vast horse herds. Moody weather didn't deter the native people who called the Wichitas home for thousands of years, and who came to regard these granite gardens of stone as a spiritual place.

The Anglos following the Indians—first military, then ranchers and farmers—tell us in their letters and journals that they were smitten by the area's uncommon beauty. A century and a half later descendants of these white settlers regard the mountains in much the same manner as the original inhabitants.

When an expatriated native son calls the Wichitas sacred ground, he's speaking from the heart. You'll hear the love in the words of writer N. Scott Momaday, a Kiowa born a few miles north of the Wichitas on the banks of Rainy Mountain Creek. You'll see the reverence in the art of Comanche Rance Hood, raised by his grandparents in the shadow of Mount Scott, one of the Wichitas' tallest. Local Kiowa and Comanche drive through the refuge to look at buffalo and remember scenes revealed to them through blood memory. In a way the Wichitas are a southern version of the South Dakota Black Hills. The Sioux lost the Black Hills, but still revere them. Places in the Wichitas provide the same spiritual resonance for the Southern Plains tribes.

The Wichita Mountains Wildlife Refuge, established in 1905 and one of the nation's oldest, has served several roles over the years. Primarily it was the place selected by bison conservationist William Temple Hornaday and President Theodore Roosevelt to reintroduce buffalo to the plains, and in doing so save the animals from extinction. Later, longhorn cattle were brought here to save that vanishing breed.

At the same time the refuge has served as an outdoor playground in a region where public lands are sparse. Over the years the Wichitas have developed a diverse fan base, from photographers who stalk bison and prairie dogs with telephoto lenses to young men and women who practice technical rock climbing on slick canyon walls in the Charon's Garden area.

Others arrive to hike, picnic, camp, fish, or simply drive through and take in the scenery. And, while a large percentage of visitors come here from Oklahoma and Texas, the appeal of the place lures travelers from throughout the country and even the world.

The refuge's popularity has made it the second-most visited in the national wildlife refuge system, averaging around a million and a half annually at this writing. Yet even with such numbers, it's easy enough to slip away into the rocks and walk for miles without seeing anything other than birds and buffalo.

A rugged little wilderness area on the west end of the refuge can, even at just 6,000 acres, swallow up the limited number of people willing to wander into this phantasmagoric jumble of granite. The trails in the wilderness mostly are the result of elk and buffalo meandering. Hiking here requires a fondness for ancient stone, and the realization that you'll have to scramble over a lot of it. The reward is solitude amid an awe-inspiring assemblage of cliffs, boulders, caves, and outcrops.

Many years ago a Comanche born in the shadow of these low mountains told me there were still secret places in the Wichitas where the commonly observed laws of nature could be reversed. For example he spoke of a waterfall that ran uphill with such reverence that who was I to doubt him?

I've been visiting the refuge for more than 40 years now, and although I've never seen a backward-flowing waterfall, there have been enough oddities of the naturally occurring variety to compensate. A little imagination is all it takes here for an out of body experience, because the land is so little changed from when George Armstrong Custer spent a day climbing Mount Scott, or when Comanche and Kiowa medicine men sent their sick to the summit of Medicine Bluff to be healed by the spirits that dwelt there.

And there's the Kiowa legend about the buffalo that retreated into the belly of Mount Scott to escape the white hide hunters and imminent extinction. It seems legend always contains a grain of truth, for after all, when it was safe, the buffalo did return to this very place. It just required some farsightedness and a new conservation ethic by those who'd exploited the wildlife resources of this fecund new world.

A travel writer once likened the refuge to places he'd visited in Africa. It had, he said, the same mix of shrubs and grass, the same spine of protruding rock, and a similar sampling of native megafauna mostly vanished from the majority of its previous range. What the Wichitas do not have is the great sweep of landscape still achievable within the African veldt. At nearly 60,000 acres, the place is large by refuge standards, yet not large enough to restore a vast Southern Plains ecotype where buffalo range in herds of thousands, not hundreds. Missing is the natural predation that once controlled wildlife population dynamics, rather than today's prescribed hunts to limit elk and deer numbers along with annual auctions that keep buffalo in balance with native range conditions.

The refuge is the size it is because in the early 1900s, President McKinley saw fit to exclude any adjoining land that was capable of supporting agriculture. The core of the refuge, officials believed, was too rocky to plow, and thus became the home of one of the nation's earliest attempts to protect species that were rapidly disappearing from the face of the earth. It was a good first step, but considering how rapidly grasslands and grassland species continue to decline, more protection as well as protection on a vastly larger scale must be a component of the region's conservation future.

A lack of scientific understanding and an ingrained European animosity towards predators resulted in several regional extinctions that can only be reversed by a conservation effort focused on size and scale. State and federal wildlife officials cooperated with area cattlemen to trap, poison, and shoot the last of the large buffalo wolves indigenous to these mountains, even in the years following the establishment of the refuge. Black bears met a similar fate, while elk native to the area were killed by hunters long before a refuge concept was even discussed. The elk population has been reintroduced, but predators will never be, due to the refuge's size and proximity to neighboring cattle ranches.

Over the course of years, federal biologists here have worked to help restore species ranging from black-capped vireos to river otters. But the rich diversity witnessed by the first traders, scouts, and cavalry officers is still missing many of its pertinent parts. What can still be found here, much as it was in 1865, is botanical integrity. Refuge managers use the same tools, bison and fire, to maintain a plant list that's been shaped by these forces since time immemorial. As a result the Wichitas, complimented by adequate rain, present a vivid flora that can be gut-wrenchingly beautiful in the spring.

The refuge has changed in the one-hundred-plus years it has served the nation's conservation effort, and there's little doubt that it will continue to change even further in the years ahead. Many of us can remember when this place was little more than an open-air funhouse for people from throughout the region and for soldiers from nearby Fort Sill. It was a rowdy crowd at times, and the resource suffered.

Today the campgrounds are fewer and better managed, a law enforcement presence keeps the obnoxious from going overboard and a state of the art visitor center reminds those who enter that the refuge system's mission is wildlife and education, a theme that's strictly enforced. As a result today's visitors are more apt to carry camera bags than party kegs, and the resource reflects this growing maturity.

Entering the Wichita Mountains Wildlife Refuge is like driving through a time warp. Visitors drive from the digital world into one little changed since the Dodge-Leavenworth Expedition first encountered Comanches near the Wichitas in the early 1800s. Scenes described by George Catlin, an artist accompanying the expedition, can still be seen here, although on a smaller scale. At the time Catlin argued for a huge grassland park to house both buffalo and Indian, so that future generations could witness the wonders he'd beheld here on the Southern Plains. The Wichita Mountains Wildlife Refuge became the nation's first tentative step. Both Catlin and the old chiefs who knew this place when it was nothing but buffalo and wilderness, would, I believe, be pleased.

In the following seasonal sketches we'll explore the Wichita Mountains as a bioregion, a wildlife refuge, a geological wonder in its own right. The Wichitas are a biological crossroads, a place where species intermingle and adapt. These mountains also have provided a stage for an important, and oftentimes tragic, chapter in the nation's history: the subjugation and internment of the Kiowa and Comanche people, for centuries the true lords of the Southern Plains.

It is a landscape that, according to the original inhabitants, once emanated power. They came to these mountains to fast, to pray, seek visions, to be cured. Today the old spirituality is overshadowed by cannons booming at nearby Fort Sill and the steady stream of traffic ascending Mount Scott. Still, the power is still here. Walk into the backcountry along a buffalo trail and much that is worrisome, frustrating, or stressful will slip away, to be replaced by the bugle of a bull elk or the steady stare of an old buffalo bull. I hope that the words that follow will help guide and inform you along the way.

January

Charon would want his overcoat this morning, or more appropriately, a buffalo robe drawn tightly around his burly shoulders as passengers lined up near his ferryboat for a final, dreaded ride.

Actually the stream is shallow enough during a dry January that I can cross in high-topped boots. The boatman's price for passage, a coin on the eye of the dead, would need to be negotiable.

Charon, for those unfamiliar with Greek mythology, is the fierce character who, according to legend, carried the souls of the deceased across the river Styx and into Hades. The artist Michelangelo portrayed him as a rugged old giant with fiery eyes and tangled hair and beard. This massive hermit in his coarse robes was said to beat the reluctant with a stout oar until they submitted and climbed aboard for a rendezvous with the not-so-distant underworld.

None of the above has much to do with a cold morning in a rocky canyon in America's heartland. But then this gash in seemingly impervious rock is, according to the map, Styx Canyon. The surrounding jumble of boulders, rock slides, and slick canyons is

JANUARY ICE. January storm coats the refuge with an inch or more of ice, breaking tree limbs and making life miserable for all but the hardiest survivors.

known as Charon's Garden, a remarkable little wilderness amid the geometrical wheat fields and county road grids that slice southwest Oklahoma into neatly accessible, sterile rectangles of agribusiness.

The wilderness area is approximately 6,000 acres of the 22,000 acres open to public use in the Wichita Mountains Wildlife Refuge, the nation's oldest. Shortly after the turn of the 20th century the refuge, some 59,000 acres in all, received several railroad cars loaded with buffalo. The animals were a gift from the New York Zoological Society, the nucleus of an effort to reestablish buffalo, or bison, on the Southern Plains after the animals were exterminated by market hunters in the late 1800s.

President Theodore "Teddy" Roosevelt, instrumental in restoring the buffalo to their prairie homeland, would be proud of the endeavor's success. A living, breathing testimonial to his vision, nearly a ton's worth, this morning stands still as statuary about 100 yards across Styx Canyon, a massive old bull occupying a small meadow in a granite amphitheater where he can eat, drink, and sleep in solitude. It's the way of the old bulls, which at some point in their advancing years choose seclusion over the social instincts natural to herd animals. Some biologists have speculated that aging bulls retreat to these remote sanctuaries as a final resting place prior to the inevitable. I've watched these old loners find a secluded spot back in the wilderness area and grow so decrepit that they struggle repeatedly to stand amid the final green pasture they've chosen to lie down in.

However on this January morning the massive bull across the canyon appears to be in good health. His ribs remain hidden behind ample flesh, a thick winter coat shining like spun gold as the sun climbs above the cedars. He pays me little mind—I believe these bulls would pay an armored U.S. Army vehicle little mind—stares for a moment, then resumes grazing as the sun paints the rock shades of pink and orange.

The Wichita Mountains exhibit some of the oldest exposed granite in the nation. The uplift occurred hundreds of millions of years ago, long enough for wind and water, freeze and thaw to sculpt the phantasmagoric rock formations that rise several hundred feet in stark contrast to the surrounding plain.

The tallest mountains in this geographic anomaly are only 2,400 feet or so above sea level. However the abrupt relief of this rugged little range, where so much barren rock seems to sprout like stone mushrooms from the surrounding grassland, gives the Wichitas character missing from other ranges much more altitude endowed. Some of the slopes feature smooth vertical faces that rock climbers appreciate. However, the major feature of Charon's Garden is the massive granite rubble, house-sized boulders scattered like pebbles tossed about carelessly by a giant.

There are boulders here as big as the recreational hot air balloons that tattoo the sky with bright colors. One rock in particular was measured at over two stories tall and 112 feet in circumference. Due to oftentimes bizarre processes of erosion, you'll find boulders with a diameter equal to that of a Merry-Go-Round perched atop granite spires much less their size, like bowling balls resting on building blocks from a child's toy box. With imagination it's not difficult to envision all this jumbled granite as a sandbox playground for some being of mythical proportions and an eye for abstract architecture.

When I was much younger I went wherever openings in the rock took me, showing little concern for the process of scrambling over boulders or searching for handholds on granite faces. But now hiking here is slower and more meditative. The wilderness area, small as it is, can test the physically vital or offer a serene resting place above a small waterfall for the age impaired. The main thing for most of us who've spent countless hours amid all this rock is the fact that you can still get lost somewhere in the middle. Small as it is, Charon's Garden, no matter if you're a serious rock climber or a seeker of spiritual enlightenment, is still wild as it gets in most modern wildlife refuges.

Styx Canyon also serves as shelter from fierce Southern Plains winds. This morning a ferocious gale blows hard and cold from the northwest, ripping across the sere plain. As a result gadwall, shoveler, and ringneck ducks have left whitecapping lakes and moved to pools in the sheltered canyons. The high temperature barely breaks 40 degrees Fahrenheit by mid-afternoon, and the low, gray cloud ceiling makes for melancholy. About the only thing cheerful in this garden of stone are flocks of cedar waxwings, khaki tan birds with yellow highlights, black masks, and jaunty feathered crests. They combat the cold by flocking through dark green junipers clinging to granite outcrops, gobbling bright blue berries.

Juniper berries are pungently astringent and an ingredient in the making of gin. They also are a winter favorite of a variety of songbirds, which consume them readily then retire to a favorite perch to digest and deploy. Avian deployment accounts for the widespread abundance of seedlings. In the Wichitas these junipers, known as red cedar, are randomly common throughout the rocks, a pleasing aspect if you're a cedar waxwing in need of calories to combat a bleak January chill.

The ducks most likely would just as soon return to the open water of the lakes dotting the refuge, where added space spells increased security. A pile of feathers along a stream bank confirms that duck was on the wild game menu recently, with some bird of prey converting waterfowl to protein. Winter in Charon's Garden is short yet serious, and hungry all the time.

Finally, by late afternoon, the sun manages to peel back the clouds just enough to allow thin light on cold, hard granite. The sun illuminates bright green moss and yellow lichen, turning drab rock into a canvas that Jackson Pollock would envy. Bright green cool season grasses are in need of an ungulate haircut along the streams, and I expect that when I leave elk will emerge from the shadows for their evening repast. Their pellet-shaped, chocolate brown calling cards are scattered everywhere I look. The droppings bring to mind a biologist who, when training wildlife management students, kept Milk Duds candy in his pocket. He'd pick up a look-a-like scat, substitute the Milk Dud hidden in his hand, take a bite, and then explain to the students that deer and elk could be sexed and their diet revealed by the flavor of their droppings.

The scruffy old whitetail doe grazing farther up in the canyon couldn't care less about biology class hi-jinks. Her job is to find enough forage to ensure both her survival and the healthy maturation of the fawn she's carrying. Nature's reproductive program is figured on a tight schedule, and it's all attuned to available nutrients. Fawns are born in spring when the vegetation is at its nutritional max, allowing for rich milk to ensure a healthy fawn's head start. At the same time the doe must have access to a diverse, quality diet so that she'll be in good breeding condition come November, forage equal to the nutritive task of compensating for low quality browse through the winter months. The good months and the meager ones must average out to provide for the both the health of the doe and the development of one or more fetuses.

The key is good habitat, and good habitat in the Wichitas ebbs and flows according to the weather. Average to ample rainfall (around 32 inches) throughout the growing season results in a well-watered mix of succulent plants, allowing for the robust health of browsers and grazers. Drought generally means lean times ahead.

The tan flank of a cow elk shows through a stand of red cedar halfway up the granite slope across Styx Canyon. She's most likely awaiting a little privacy before coming out to the edge of the meadow to graze on dormant grama grasses. She needs the calories and I need to get out of the up-and-down granite and onto the level plain before sundown. A great blue heron soars over the ridge and then drops like a military glider down to one of the canyon's pools, the water reflecting a pewter sheen in failing light.

Cold weather retreats for a few days, and the pools in the canyons have warmed enough that by mid-afternoon swarms of midges hover near the water like puffs of smoke. The winged insects are tiny, not much bigger than a capital M in this text, but plentiful on sunny afternoons when the temperature climbs above forty.

Tiny insects on the wing invite winged predators, and even now, in the coldest month of the year, a dragonfly is on the prowl. Clear wings, a reddish abdomen, and a flight period that sometimes extends through the winter suggest one of the meadowhawks, possibly a variegated meadowhawk, a dragonfly noted for tolerating cold temperatures.

Streamside thickets, a mix of elm and cedar laced together by prickly strands of greenbrier, play host to a songbird convention of drab gray titmice and juncos, plus bright crimson cardinals. Streamside grasses display their native prairie heritage in winter shades of orange and straw yellow—little bluestem, switchgrass, Indian grass, dropseed, and ankle-high clumps of blue grama. Creek pools are tap water clear, the streamside stone bright red-orange and smooth as glass due to untold centuries of cascading current. Water striders skate over the surface film, their spider-like shadows resembling tiny kittens' paws.

Under the soft glare of slanted winter sunlight, slow-moving minnows flash like signal mirrors as they twist from side to side while grazing on the olive green algae or gleaning some microscopic animal prey. The pools also play host to snails with oval shells the same olive color as the algae. Pale white bodies, heads and antennae extend from the shells, and the slow-moving gastropods graze the elysian fields of algae much like the buffalo graze the adjacent prairie grasses.

Dark water beetles, either diving from or returning to the surface to store oxygen for another plunge, search the pool for detritus to scavenge. A waterfall flows over a granite ledge, drops four feet and adds oxygen to the water. The afternoon is closing in on sixty degrees and life, large and small, insect, mammal, reptile and amphibian, is responding. Late in the afternoon a tiny chorus frog calls tentatively, almost as if the time has arrived to practice upcoming spring vocals.

Ample moisture and unseasonable January warmth have spurred the growth of wild rye grasses shaded by steep canyon walls, and scattered elk pellets big as the first joint of my thumb vouch for the horse-sized animals' approval of this succulent food source. The fact that green forage is available shows in the moistness of the elk droppings. Dry forage would result in scat of corncob consistency rather than something as pliable as these pellets, each easily flattened between forefinger and thumb. The rye grasses will mature and set seed while the warm season natives are just entering their explosive spring growth. For the cool season grasses, it's an adaptation allowing the species to get a jump on the competition. For elk, it's manna from the mountaintops.

Elk in the refuge are the result of a restoration process that began in earnest in 1911. That's when a bull and four cow elk were taken from a herd in Jackson, Wyoming, and released to join another bull elk already on the grounds, a loner donated by refuge patrons from Wichita, Kansas.

The following year 15 additional elk were shipped south from Wyoming, and these animals became the predecessors of the modern refuge herd. The transplant has proven so successful that the animals require periodic culling, and enough have slipped out of the refuge to establish thriving herds in adjacent counties on privately owned ranches and farms.

My first encounter with Wichita Mountains elk resulted in an epic adrenalin rush. A friend and I, on an October camping trip, found a rusty old hand pump near the Elk Mountain area, and late one evening we set about filling several water jugs.

Each stroke of the pump handle resulted in a clear, cold, stream of water accompanied by a loud mechanical squeak. Within minutes the noisy pump was answered by a much more impressive high-pitched squeal, an invitation to do battle from 700 pounds of enraged flesh belonging to an extremely irate bull elk.

The bull's "bugle" was as overpowering as a tugboat's foghorn. He'd scream, turn his massive antlers to the task of disassembling some small post oak or red cedar in his path, advance and once again vent his anger with an audible screech that carried like a steam engine whistle.

By the time the bull burst out of the timber ready to do battle with the water pump, he was less than 30 yards away. Massive antlers were festooned with limbs, twigs, cedar boughs and dirt. The big guy was in a rage, ready to thrash this upstart pump that sounded so much like a rival. And there we stood, mouths agape, staring into the inflamed eyes of wild nature.

That bull soon decided he'd been duped and stalked away to check on any cows that might be sequestered in the post oaks. His upcoming days were destined to be more of the same: lusting, fighting, grazing, napping, and passing his magnificent genes on to elk generations that followed.

One of the first documented encounters with Wichita Mountains elk occurred in 1869, when General Phillip Sheridan of Civil War and Indian fighting fame arrived at nearby Fort Sill, on a mission to eradicate the last of the defiant Southern Plains tribes. Sheridan, a remorseless soldier, loved to hunt as much as he loved victory on the field of battle. The general and his contingent rode to a partially wooded, secluded area west of Mount Scott, where they killed five animals described as Merriam's elk, a species once common to the desert mountains of Arizona, Texas, and New Mexico but hunted into extinction before the turn of the 20th century.

Biologist/natural historian Art Halloran claimed that the last of the Wichitas's original elk fell to a hunter's bullet near Rainy Mountain in 1881. Rainy Mountain is a small mound amid a vast prairie north of the refuge and once a favorite camping place for the Kiowa tribe.

Early explorers in the area noted that the slopes of Elk Mountain, a dominant landmark in the wilderness area, were strewn with elk antlers when they first visited. Although elkless for some 30 years, it appears that the Wichitas always were excellent elk habitat and remain so today, judging from the explosive recolonization and the amount of culling authorized every year to keep the number of animals in sync with available living quarters.

Sadly, several species native to the refuge were destroyed before predecessors of today's U.S. Fish & Wildlife Service arrived to save them. The buffalo were a gift from the New York Zoological Society and rode the railways back to their former range. Turkeys were restored with birds captured from Texas. An attempt at returning pronghorn antelope to the refuge was half-hearted and unsuccessful.

On the other hand, several tough and wily predators were frustratingly difficult to eradicate, given that early in the refuge's history the elimination of bears and wolves was considered mandatory. According to Halloran the last four bears in the Wichitas were killed in 1934. The war on gray wolves in the region was ruthless and effective. Halloran reported that the last lobo was hunted down and killed early in the century, probably 1906. However rumors of resident wolves hiding out in the mountains persisted until the mid-1930s.

Cougars occasionally reveal themselves in the refuge, the last of the large predators once common here. These eroded mountains have been called an island in a prairie sea, and the refuge itself remains an island amid an ocean of crops and ranchland. Ranchers and farmers have little use for predators disrespectful enough to occasionally dine on livestock, and although the refuge may seem large at 59,000 acres, the amount of land is tiny compared to the needs of, say, a wolf pack. Large predators stake out large territories, and wolves roaming beyond refuge boundaries would raise a howl heard as far away as Washington D.C.

So thank God for cougars, or at least the notion of them. The country here is rugged enough to make you think that a big cat could be anywhere. I've never seen one in the Wichitas, nor seen sign. However, refuge staff report sightings, and it's not hard to believe that something tawny and lithe, a secretive animal weighing nearly 200 pounds with powerful jaws and rapier teeth, could be watching. The presence of a cougar or even the possibility of one keeps the wilderness barometer from dipping too far into the comfort zone. The wilderness of the mind needs something stealthy sharing space, something with the ability to bite back, and cougars more than qualify.

As part of the former Kiowa and Comanche Indian reservations, the mountains protected within the refuge remain much as they were before white settlement. Tales of gold for the taking led to a turn-of-the-20th century mini-rush that lasted several years and left the area pocked with shallow excavations bordered by piles of granite gravel, places where prospectors chipped away in search of gold. Most of the diggings are shallow, representing a few days worth of very hard labor. The digs were soon abandoned for other locations that somehow promised to be better than the last, leaving sweat-stained trails of diggings in each miner's fortune-crazed wake.

Over the years the Wichitas have accumulated a hearty folklore of treasure tales, including rumors of Spanish booty and of outlaws who buried loot in the rough country that now comprises Charon's Garden. The original waves of gold seekers arrived driven by rumors of old Spanish mines and nuggets for the picking. Eventually the miners were chased out of the area when the Wichitas were declared first a forest preserve and then a national wildlife refuge. Today the abandoned digs fill with water following spring rains and play host to leopard frogs, while modern-day treasure hunters comb the canyons and dream of lost fortune left behind by outlaws like Jesse James.

The warm spell continues for several more days, with afternoon temperatures in the seventies. The refuge, not far from the Red River forming the Oklahoma/Texas border, lies far enough south to experience springlike weather throughout the winter, and several days with highs around seventy and lows in the forties have resulted in an untimely spring bouquet. A patch of verbena with dark green leaves and purple flowers is in bloom at the base of a granite slope facing the sun-drenched south. Unfortunately the plant is flowering at least two months early, and will be destined to suffer severe frostbite when a cold front slams down out of the north within a week's time.

Yet, for several days at least, the Wichitas are staging a spring preview. Overwintering butterflies are out roaming this afternoon, one of them smallish, orange and brown and gone before I can identify it, the other an orange sulfur, fluttering under the sun on pale yellow wings sporting black tips. Later in the afternoon a questionmark butterfly cruises above a small creek, the insect's rich red-orange wings out of place amid all the winter drab. Clouds of midges rise above a creek near where a red-shafted flicker probing for insect larvae rotates around the trunk of a dead elm. Just at dusk an armadillo wanders into a meadow, stopping to root amid the tussocks of little bluestem. A pile of blue jay feathers is all that remains of the bird's encounter with a Cooper's hawk. Background music revs up courtesy of Strecker's chorus frogs, voices still tentative for the time being as they await more substantial signs of spring.

By the following weekend the weather has indulged itself in another abrupt Southern Plains change of heart. The temperature fights to reach the mid-thirties with clouds hanging low, gray and heavy as spitting rain freezes on the mountaintops, where fog gathers atop flesh-colored granite like a gray woolen watch cap. This time it's a goldeneye duck that's sought out a canyon pool for shelter from the wind. A striped skunk, waddling across the prairie, appears unconcerned with the sudden change of weather, while a small flock of Rio Grande wild turkeys scours a small grove of post oaks in hopes that a few acorns may still be scattered beneath the brown, leathery leaf litter. Buffalo and elk graze together on the open prairie, comfortable in their winter coats. A break in the clouds allows a shaft of sunlight to illuminate a twisted dead cedar perched on a point of rock overlooking a small stream. The image is almost biblical; "Jesus light," photographers call it, when multiple beams break through dark clouds like the searchlights at an airport turned upside down. The old cedar is only a one-armed cross, but it suffices to serve the illusion. If this were a Cecil B. DeMille movie, a dramatic score would erupt behind the visual magnificence. Right on cue, a canyon wren riddles the granite with a bubbling, tumbling, reverberating burst of sheer joy.

The rain and light freeze is mild compared to weather that will follow. Snow and ice intensify, and the temperature rarely rises above freezing. All of the refuge's residents concentrate on eating and not being eaten. The latter is a simple task for buffalo, elk, and deer now that the wolves are gone. However for rabbits, squirrels, rats, and mice, it's a dance dangerously near the edge. Hunger is an insistent temptress, urging a mouse into a clearing it might normally avoid. At the same time the ears, eyes, and noses of predators ranging from coyote to fox, bobcat to owl are honed exceptionally keen by the prospects of starvation.

January is a tough time to making a living in the wild, especially for juvenile predators. Living on the strength of tooth, talon, and claw is the result of a learning experience, and only the best survive the trial and error classroom. Few first-year predators remain around to celebrate their initial birthday.

With predators, experience is the best ticket to survival. On this overcast afternoon an adult sharp-shinned hawk perches on a solitary boulder amid several hundred acres of prairie left patchy by partially melted snow. The alert little bird, blue-gray with a white breast marked with reddish streaking, engages a stare that's so intense it seems a laser beam will suddenly shoot out of a searing red eye and illuminate a well-worn rodent trail leading from one brown grass clump to another.

The hawk is a bundle of feathered energy, and won't wait for good fortune to appear on its own. In a second the bird is back on the wing, a portrait of concentrated motion, primed to take a single, small brown sparrow from a larger flock that scatters when feathers explode in the wintry air. The scene appears commonplace to a coyote trotting across the prairie. The old song dog is licking his lips over dark mice silhouetted against white snow, winter repast that will make the night seem much less chilly.

It's been a cold January for the Southern Plains, with temperatures below normal and ice and snow above. A golden eagle has taken over a bare-limbed cottonwood near a prairie dog town not far from the wilderness area. The eagle scans the prairie with its magnificent eyesight, and I'm sure that prairie dog served on the rare side would make the big bird's day a perfect one. I flush a red-tailed hawk from its kill along a trail leading into the backcountry. All that remains of the cottontail rabbit is the hide, entrails, and a bloody hind leg. My first thought is that the hawk had a successful hunt, and I hope it will return in due time to finish liver and lights. However, redtails are as quick to scavenge as they are to hunt, and it's possible that the rabbit died of old age, injuries, or illness.

At daybreak a row of cottonwoods along a stream greets the sun with rim ice gleaming like polished silver where fog still clings to upper branches and twigs. Overhead a flock of Canada geese have abandoned their overnight quarters on some nearby lake to fly low and noisily to a winter wheat field and breakfast.

Ledges along streams, especially in the canyons that see little sunlight this time of year, wear belated Christmas ornaments. Icicles from several inches to several feet long dangle from places where water drips. Below the ledges are frozen waterfalls holding back frozen riffles and waves. Below all this hoary artistry a steady stream of water continues to flow unimpeded beneath ice tapestries that beg for a backdrop of northern lights, even here in the mostly sunny south.

Several hundred yards away a bachelor group of bull bison grazes on short stemmed, straw-colored blue grama cleared of snow by wind and intermittent sun. Fog has capped the mountains the past several mornings, and though the temperature at daybreak remains at or near freezing, the afternoons have warmed into the sixties.

At mid-afternoon a large flock of turkeys strolls through the pink and tan grasses, pecking at seeds and maybe even an occasional grasshopper. It's always seemed amazing that, following an ice storm or blizzard, grasshoppers are back catapulting from the grass as soon as the sun warms. A bobcat, resting on its haunches at the edge of an oak grove, cares little about grasshoppers when turkeys are on the radar screen. The beautiful little wildcat, fur in winter prime in shades of tan, brown, russet, and gray, stares at the turkeys as if it will simply wish them into pouncing distance, feline mind definitely concentrated on a drumstick.

Throughout the month groups of whitetail does have wandered far from timber each morning, gathering in the prairies to graze or browse. Something in the grass has caught their attention and stoked their appetites, maybe the low-growing winter rosettes of some favorite forb. A few plants in the refuge retain green basal growth throughout the winter, ready to begin explosive growth as soon as the sun climbs and spring rains relay an opportune signal to launch.

The deer are lovely in their gray winter coats, a shade complimenting the silver gray of an adult male northern harrier that drifts on outstretched wings a few feet over the grass, ready to drop and devour a mouse before it's aware that the airways have turned deadly. Not far from a prairie dog town a flock of longspurs arise due to some unseen commotion, form a flock and twist and turn in unison as if under the command of electronic remote control. The birds cruise at an altitude corresponding to the lay of the land, serenading prairie dogs with a bright musical twitter.

The short warming trend makes for a nice day to walk West Cache Creek in search of river otters. Otters were reintroduced here several years ago and, according to refuge personnel, the transplants from Louisiana have managed to make a go of it. The charismatic members of the weasel family occupy old beaver burrows and, although not readily seen, are known by their calling card of scat comprised of fish scale concentrate.

It's a perfect afternoon for scat searching if not for otter spotting. Instead, visual rewards arrive courtesy of winter waterfowl clustered on the creek pools. By mid-afternoon the stream is brimming with Canada geese plus gadwalls in their mousey gray and brown plumage. A natty widgeon drake, an artist's palette of pink, blue, gray, brown, and white, proves that nature can blend colors that would cause an art teacher to shudder. However the afternoon prize is a canvasback drake, a king-sized diving duck that's absolutely regal with red head, white body and black breast and tail. The canvasback is a duck that looks as if it has been outfitted by a fussy British tailor. A waterfowler's prize, the canvasback also earns bonus points for edibility.

Beaver have been busy along West Cache Creek. Fresh stumps and pale wood chips from streamside trees and shrubbery are common along the trail bordering the refuge's largest stream. A bluff along the south bank isn't particularly high, maybe 30 feet, but in January casts enough shadow to ensure that the south edge of the stream remains encased in ice while the north bank is mostly muddy.

Somewhere overhead a flock of sandhill cranes chatters while flying out to graze on farm crops. Voices combine to form a high, wild whinny, a song that has enthralled some of the nation's greatest poets, writers, and conservationists. The crane choir carries well enough to outperform the raucous blue jays assembled in the oak, walnut, elm, and pecan trees clustered along the narrow stream terrace. Judging from the piles of neatly stripped blue feathers beneath the trees, it appears that these blue jays should forego a little brashness and concentrate more on predator detection.

Snow and ice from previous weeks has pruned the numerous red cedars growing between the larger hardwoods. The pruning has left a green carpet of juniper twigs, allowing for a quiet walk spiced by an aroma that can't be bottled and sold. Ahead a kingfisher chatters, then dives like a winged rock, surfacing seconds later with a hard earned minnow. By the time I've returned to the trailhead, swarms of tiny midges are dancing over the stream, reflecting sunlight like some wind spun zephyr. Redheaded woodpeckers search for beetle larvae under the peeling bark of a dying elm while I memorize the mental snapshot that serves as my going-away present—a salute from a flicker headed upstream on an undulating flight path, a handsome bird that flashes a quick glimpse of salmon underwing in its passing.

It has been a January in need of an encore, a dramatic curtain call for a month of unusual snow, ice, and cold temperatures. By the end of the month the final act is a winter storm that ravages the land with unrelenting frozen fury.

The storm arrives with light rain that freezes as the temperature drops into the twenties. By the time the precipitation ends, everything is coated with ice, in places an accumulation of two inches or more.

A cold fog persists throughout the following day, and the weight of the ice brings trees or parts of trees crashing to the ground. Many of the larger oaks within the refuge split in two at the bases of major branches. Saplings encased in ice are bent over by the weight, crowns resting on the ground.

Red cedars, evergreens that retain their needle-like leaves in winter, appear as if ice has been sprayed over the boughs with an airbrush. Some are shattered, some flattened by the weight. Even the prairie grasses are sheathed in ice, so much so that it's a struggle to walk through patches of knee-high bluestem.

A prairie dog town resembles a skating rink. Most of the inhabitants remain underground to ride out the weather, but a few pups are out sliding around on the slick white surface, probably hoping for a tourist to happen along with a bag of popcorn. One of the young rodents waddles up to a kneeling photographer and places both front paws on his leg, as if beseeching him to make this deadly frozen world turn warm again.

Meadowlarks hanging around the periphery of the dog town seem to be in shock, most likely weakened by the inability to scavenge seeds. An ice storm of this magnitude makes it nearly impossible for birds to forage, and some will die of hunger or become easy prey. At the same time it's lovely weather for the adult Cooper's hawk, similar in appearance to its sharp-shinned cousin, yet larger. This one, a particularly beautiful angel of death, perches on a singular shrub enshrouded in several inches of ice amid a large prairie meadow that gleams as white as a winter mountaintop in Montana. The hawk scrutinizes the landscape with a practiced eye, and I remember the bright yellow breasts of those hapless meadowlarks.

The ice lingers and both predators and prey abandon any pretense other than survival. Barred owls are in plain sight in trees and atop stumps along streams, firmly planted in place and showing little inclination to flee when I stop nearby and fumble for a camera. Whitetail does feed throughout the day in oak groves that look like the aftermath of an artillery battle. One young doe is perfectly framed by icy winter leaves as she samples available fare, nibbling at the tip of a shrub then turning to trim foliage from a juniper.

Buffalo graze throughout the afternoon, and it's evident why evolution has provided them with massive heads. The animals butt away the ice and manage a mouthful of grass, especially the dormant grama and buffalo grasses that retain nutrients throughout the winter. The older bulls swing heads that appear to be the size of small Volkswagens, and all endure the weather with patent buffalo patience. Bison equanimity endears these animals to those of us not quite so blessed. It's a live demonstration of how the bison tribe mastered life here on these once great American grasslands, an environment duly noted for its fickle weather.

By late afternoon the fog has become so thick that buffalo thirty yards distant appear as hazy ghosts up to their hocks in white ice held in place by a ground-hugging, gray blanket. A small band of elk materializes on a hilltop for a second. Then their pale winter outerwear dissolves into the fog, swallowed up by the worst of winter. The temperature holds in the low twenties and it's easy to envision ice locked in place until May. But in reality a south wind will arrive in a day or so and restore the landscape in a matter of hours. For now there's little joy here where the buffalo roam, a sentiment best expressed by a coyote chorus so mournful that even the buffalo raise their heads and focus on the dirge, as if the blues hour had just started playing on the radio.

The surreal scene made me think of the first time I'd seen the refuge under a blanket of ice and snow. It was in the early 1970s, and the whiteness reminded me of a Christmas card featuring a snowman and children at play. But this was different. I'd been coming to the refuge since 1969, helped with elk hunts while working for the Oklahoma wildlife department, assisted with Youth Conservation Corps kids building trails, rock climbed with my brother when both of us were much younger and thinner, sold stories about the refuge to both regional and national magazines and newspapers, hiked for the sheer pleasure of it off and on for more than 40 years, and kept field notes dating back to the early 1980s. And during all that time I'd never seen a winter storm like this one. This was the kind of storm that would change both the face and the biological complexity of the area for years to come. And then, a little more than a year later, the refuge would be ravaged by the worst drought in its history, a drought accompanied by record high temperatures that helped spawn uncontrollable wildfires throughout the eastern half of the refuge.

So it seemed that weather events in the Wichitas hadn't deviated much from the norm for decades, then suddenly unleashed a brutal rampage of fire and ice. The weather moods here tend to bare their teeth when angered, I thought as I drove past a utility pole snapped in two by the weight of the ice. Somebody needs to go to the top of the mountain, and have a long and apologetic talk.

February

Last night striped skunks were on the prowl, evidenced by the number of carcasses along the roads leading into the refuge. It's skunk breeding season and the animals haven't learned that a glandular chemical defense system won't deter a charging automobile. Those that survive great horned owls and vehicular carnage will be responsible for a new generation of young skunks in about two months' time. But, for now, a striped skunk roadside rendezvous oftentimes results in crow carrion.

February in the Wichitas is a month that can't quite figure itself out. It's as if winter is frantically straining to keep the door closed as spring shoves from the other side. Generally by mid-month the first tiny bluets and spring beauties can be found pushing up through oak leaf litter. Early in the month the upper branches of wild plum, bois d'arc, and willow show a flush of awakening in tones of dark purple, lemon yellow, and orange. The frog chorus increases in both numbers and volume as February melds into March and birds start chattering about nesting territory.

WINTER WHITETAIL. Refuge deer turn to low quality browse like eastern red cedar when snow and ice limit winter foraging.

Then a winter storm blows in and spring's advance stays on hold until the south winds return. As soon as the landscape warms up a few degrees the bluebirds are back in nesting mode and the little chorus frogs are calling from ephemeral pools. The desire to reproduce is once again building to a crescendo, and a few bitter days are more of a recess than a deterrent.

However, during this particular winter the abnormal snow and ice of January have taken a toll. An oak grove halved by a small intermittent stream holds what's left of an elk. The animal died next to a shallow pool, and this is where the coyotes have come to feast. Little remains other than scattered hair and freshly chewed bones, mostly legs and ribs, and a mangled hide that will soon be shredded by any number of large and small appetites.

In time the remains will be reduced to residue as the drama of life and death grows increasingly focused on renewal. Strecker's chorus frogs, largest of the chorus frog tribe and among the earliest breeders, have moved into the small granite pools of a seasonal stream tumbling down from the Charon's Garden highlands. The largest pools are approximately three and a half feet in diameter, six to eight inches deep and lined with finely ground granite gravel that shines like gold when the sun breaks through a low overcast.

The little frogs, about an inch and a half long, are calling from clumps of grass that grew in the pools as they dried up last summer. Now the tips extend just above the waterline, providing calling perches and egg-laying structure. The water is cold and the frogs are darker than the buff and reddish brown shades that predominate in warmer weather. One of the males is a dark gray-bluish green mixture, others a blend of gray and brown earth tones.

A male about the size of a silver dollar seeks to summon a mate while floating in a shallow pool. Another rides a thin grass stem that's bent over from the tiny amphibian's weight, the tip barely touching the water. The vocals are riveting even if choir members tend to be on the small side.In fact the entire length of the canyon echoes with Strecker's chorus frog music, the vocals like a high-pitched whistle from a distance, but coarser and in noticeable couplets when standing closer to the source.

The chorus frogs choose these temporary pools due to the absence of predatory fish. Stocky little Strecker's, which tend to look somewhat chubby with forelegs that resemble the arms of a Sumo wrestler, breed opportunistically when the water temperature resisters between 35 to 70 degrees Fahrenheit. Females make their way from under rocks and out of burrows to the breeding pools, ready to shed clumps of eggs while clasped by an amorous male. Fertilized egg clumps are attached to aquatic plants and twigs, and a single female may lay up to 700 eggs in 75 separate clumps. If conditions are conducive, the eggs may hatch in as little as a week, and the tadpoles race to metamorphose before the pools dry up at the end of spring rains.

Another among the refuge's common winter anthems is the loud cawing of crows intent on crow mischief. Mostly this entails the harassment of hawks and owls that happily dine on crow at every opportunity. Crows repay such effrontery by daylight mobbing that involves as many crows as can be summoned by caws and throaty growls.

Crows have a sinister reputation that belies their above-average intelligence. The bad rap has more to due with errant folklore than anything the birds have actually done to engender the wrath of *Homo sapiens*. Winter owl mobbing congregations appear to represent an influx of adolescent crows eager to raise crow hell.But then it's easy to anthropomorphize these crafty birds with an I.Q. that might embarrass Old Rover and may rank with nonhuman primates.

I've watched ravens play orchestrated games on elementary school playground equipment, and the rules appeared to be as complex as those employed by fifth graders. *National Geographic* reports that members of the Corvid family routinely use tools, including the wisdom to let automobiles do the work of cracking hard-shelled nuts like walnuts and pecans. The birds have learned to drop the nuts into roadways at traffic lights, then wait patiently for the light to change before retrieving their efficiently cracked booty.

So it's easy to surmise that the owl mobbing is the result of crow rage at some cousin having been picked off a perch in the depth of darkness. Unfortunately crows also suffer indignities at the hand of man, including attempts at outright elimination, especially the elimination of large winter roosts. Considering ongoing research that illuminates crow intelligence in brightly favorable new light, it now seems that the grudge held towards our Corvid neighbors may have stemmed from simple jealousy.

This morning's crow din was ignited by a nervous-appearing great horned owl that's taken refuge in a post oak grove. The morning stillness that follows the departing crows amplifies leaf scratching by a spotted towhee searching for spiders beneath the oaks. If not for the low cloud cover the day would be springlike, a factor not lost on yellow sulfur butterflies and drab brown dragonflies darting about on the wing by early afternoon. A bright orange and black lady beetle rests on a shrub beside the trail, a tiny harbinger of the wide variety of insect life that will be commonplace here in a few weeks' time.

Lady beetles, ladybug beetles, ladybird beetles or just plain ladybugs are among the few insects that most people recognize and view with favor. The most common lady beetles in the refuge are *Hippodamia convergens*, the convergent ladybug. These pill-sized, orange and black-spotted insects are predacious on aphids and moth eggs, and are the common ladybug sold to gardeners as a natural deterrent to aphids.

In the Southwest, convergent ladybugs are known for the tremendous aggregations found atop the "sky island" mountains that tower above the desert. *Arizona Highways Magazine* once ran a story pointing out that convergent ladybugs "descend on Arizona mountaintops every year, turning trees, rocks and shrubs into quivering orange chimeras."

According to the magazine, entomologists estimate that by midsummer, populations can reach concentrations of 120 million per acre. The article added that no one knows for sure why the insects take part in this massive migration to mountaintops, since the peaks don't offer a particularly good source of aphids. Some believe a combination of temperature and humidity attracts the ladybugs. Others postulate that the beetles may be drawn by olfactory incentives.

Whatever the enticement, it results in a lot of ladybugs. Entomologists explain that once they've set up camp on the mountaintops, the insects feed on pollen, which stimulates hormones that make the ladybugs groggy. As a consequence they tend to snooze away the days.

By late autumn the ladybugs are huddled together, prepared to overwinter. When spring arrives the beetles become active, find a mate from among the millions, then fly down the mountain in search of aphids. A feast of her favorite food results in eggs laid, which signals the end of Mrs. Ladybug. Eggs hatch within a week, larvae go in search of aphids, and the cycle begins anew.

Once, atop King Mountain, third highest in the Wichitas and the last big mountain at the western end of the range, I found a mass of convergent ladybugs that matched the description in *Arizona Highways*. Granite boulders and bedrock were covered with ladybugs, so many that the mountaintop appeared to have been spray painted bright orange. This was in early June and the scene resembled a vast canvas of abstract art, including pink and orange granite streaked with gray, green, and yellow lichen and then smothered with a mass of squirming orange and black ladybug beetles. The Arizona entomologists would have, I believe, felt right at home atop King Mountain. It was among the most awe-inspiring sights I've encountered in the Wichitas, and proof that, in nature, the biblical adage "seek, and ye shall find" oftentimes results in unexpected dividends.

The slopes of King Mountain that year wore a bright yellow blanket of flowering coreopsis, enough, it seems in retrospect, to keep millions of ladybugs groggy. As for aphids, I'm sure the surrounding cropland offered up a smorgasbord, but unfortunately the heavy applications of pesticides that keep farmers in business wouldn't differentiate between beloved ladybugs and hated aphids.

Along a trail in the refuge's Charon's Garden area there's a post oak tree that rises straight up several feet before bending at a right angle. The angle is almost perfectly aligned to form a universal buffalo back-scratching post—so much so that over the years the underside of the trunk, the part parallel to the ground, has been worn smooth as glass by bison with an itch that needs tending.

It's a good place to find clumps of shed buffalo wool in the springtime, and not far from a small, stair-stepping stream that on this particular afternoon hosts a number of crayfish on the move, each a pale brownish green with orange markings and ranging from an inch to three inches or more in length.

A bright orange millipede has sequestered a sunny spot in some parched grass, which now offers new shoots at the base of scattered clumps. The new grass grows green in places that receive adequate sunlight, while gray and white patches of snow survive where sunlight-blocking granite outcrops result in additional hours of deep shade. Elk seek the new green growth; they have subsisted on hay cured on the stem for several months now, and the grazers come out of the shelter of post oak groves to feed in their tattered winter coats.

In February the elk are as pale as the dried grass they've been munching. The saddle area is light tan to almost white, contrasting the darker brown of necks, legs, and heads. Bulls still wear their battle gear prior to shedding, and the antlers are polished and shine in the sun like ivory. One of the bulls feeding in a prairie meadow has an antler broken off about halfway down from autumn's jousting, while another sports a rack with tines grown together to form a "shovel" that would look at home on a caribou. The elk appear ragged and ready to shed all this winter hair, and at times somewhat uncomfortable in weather with high temperatures in the 50s, strong south winds and overcast skies. The days are growing longer now, and soon dark green sedges will appear in moist, low areas, a gift from reemerging hours of sunlight and the stream of moisture riding the wind currents north from the Gulf of Mexico.

A chance meeting with some refuge personnel provides interesting news. They report four active otter dens along a refuge stream. I spend the afternoon looking for otters, and while the search reveals what appears to be otter scat, I have no luck in finding the animal that left such a tantalizing clue. However the hike does reveal several Townsend's solitaires, robin-sized, long-tailed gray birds with distinctive white eye rings. The solitaires are east of their regular western Rocky Mountains range, and thus a good find for bird watchers. Most likely they're here to dine on juniper berries, a winter favorite.

Late in February a walk along Little Medicine Creek left me with the impression that the refuge has gone to the hogs. Several feral pigs (domesticated hogs gone wild) are surprised while rooting along a stream, and the damage they leave behind resembles the aftermath of an encounter with a garden tiller.

Hog damage throughout the refuge increased during the early years of the 21st century, as the animals expanded their territory at an alarming rate. Many of these disease harboring, habitat-destroying invaders are the result of domestic animals released for hunters to shoot. Feral hogs generally prove to be almost impossible to eradicate once established, due to high birth rates.

In the Wichitas the hogs tend to root so efficiently that they literally push back the shallow soils on grassy granite outcrops. In places it appears as if the sod has been rolled up like a rug as the animals rummage for roots, insects or whatever else is pleasing to a feral pig's palette. These glade areas contain some of the most interesting plant communities in the refuge and remain among the most fragile, and it seems a travesty that encroaching hogs can invade and inflict such extensive damage, all because a few hunters tend to confuse domestic animals with "wild Russian boars."

The pigs that have invaded the Wichitas are plain old barnyard pigs. However life in the wild has changed the animals' appearance, from pleasing bacon makers to something a bit more sinister. Domestic hogs, following several generations back in the wild, become leaner, grow bristly dark coats and in time begin to look as tough and savvy as their Russian counterparts, or enough so to fulfill the fantasies of gunners seeking dangerous game. On the other hand, state and federal wildlife officials see them for what they are—a scourge. The destruction is so comprehensive at times that all one can do is daydream of an eradicating airstrike from nearby Fort Sill.

Pigs are a pestilence inflicting long-term environmental damage that's readily apparent to biologists and land-use novices alike. Invasive plants, like some of the bromes that mature early in spring, are both difficult to eradicate and hard to recognize, unlike the pigs. The damage they do is subtle, yet also results in the overall degradation of the refuge's biological integrity. About the only way to resist the advances of either is by maintaining good land health. Over the years, biologists have sought to keep the biological system in good working order by reestablishing native species, like buffalo and elk. They also trap and destroy the aliens, like domestic pigs, and ensure a healthy relationship between those that eat and that which is eaten by keeping the numbers of consumers within the carrying capacity of the land. Some animals are hunted, some are trapped and sold, with the end result a healthy grassland renewed periodically with simple yet essential tools like fire. The next step involves a leap of faith, and requires a prayer that the rains arrive in a timely fashion. Spring rains that can begin as early as February are essential to retaining grassland health. When the rains don't come the plant communities retreat into dormancy, and the buffalo wish the fences were down so they could return to the old days and the old ways, and migrate in search of a few dark clouds.

The final week in February arrives with warm west winds, a turquoise sky that would make New Mexico proud, and a fringe-like halo of white clouds rimming the mountains. The stage for spring is set with streams clear and flowing, wild plums beginning to flower, and bright purple clumps of verbena near a pool bordered by elms with enlarged, rusty brown flower buds.

Refuge personnel are beginning their spring controlled burns to stimulate grass growth, control the spread of woody vegetation and create a mosaic of grazing patterns throughout the refuge. Buffalo and longhorn cattle congregate on the burned areas, allowing adjacent grassland to develop increased leafy surface area, store nutrients, and rest. In future years the rested areas are burned, the recently burned allowed to rest, ad infinitum. It's a pattern and process as old as the prairie itself, first practiced by native nomads who used fire to concentrate game animals. Without fire and grazing pressure, native grasslands would become brushy savannah and eventually, a spindly forest that might support whitetail deer, but would spell doom for large grazers.

Frog tadpoles are active in streams as the temperature climbs, and graceful clumps of trout lilies grow amid secluded rocky basins.

The flowers are white, the fleshy leaves a soft blue-green with darker mottling. Bluebirds call from a tree with a hollow cavity caused by an ice storm that snapped off a large limb. A granite ledge streaked with yellow lichen extends over the pool, a perfect perch for an eastern phoebe to watch for emerging aquatic insects.

For the past several days the afternoon high temperatures have reached the low sixties, and some of the elms begin to flower. The tiny red flowers are inconspicuous and mostly wind pollinated. A flock of song sparrows, white breasts heavily streaked with brown, are active in the thick winter grass along a stream. One hundred yards away, a prairie meadow displays a spiny plum thicket as a centerpiece. A flock of vesper sparrows has found the dense shrubbery attractive. The binocular-wielding onlooker finds the birds, with their white eye rings and russet wing patches, attractive as well.

By late afternoon the wind has grown light and the birds even more active. Rufus-crowned sparrows have joined song and vesper on the checklist. Grasshoppers flush from bleached brown grass, and dark brown mourning cloaks, orange questionmarks, and yellow sulfur butterflies cruise while chorus frogs crank up the volume and a squadron of sandhill cranes croon their poignant anthem overhead. A new longhorn calf hugs the flanks of a skinny mother cow, and a red-bellied woodpecker taps out a staccato territorial warning from a post oak grove. Bluets and spring beauties flower underfoot, and the fernlike leaves of yarrow are pushing up through rapidly warming prairie earth. As dusk approaches I find a shed elk antler that's been chewed and converted into calcium by one of the refuge rodents. A flock of rusty red and brown field sparrows with their pinkish bills exit a scrimpy savannah of stunted blackjack oaks, while several of last spring's buffalo calves take over a prairie dog town for a round of butting, bucking, rolling in the mud, and basically being young on a day perfectly made for it. The cow buffalo, on the other hand, ignore the youngsters' antics and show their appreciation for this teasing taste of spring by grazing whatever new shoots of green grass that are available.

February here is schizoid month, with days that reach 80 degrees, nights that can drop down to eight above zero. Sometimes such extremes happen on the same day. Some of the region's heaviest snows have been recorded in late February and early March, while other years have been so warm that new green leaves pop out on trees—generally much to the tree's chagrin, for the average date of the final freeze here is still weeks away. Fortunately there are auxiliary buds for trees teased into leafing out early.

Still, the sun is climbing a little higher in the southern sky, the days are a little longer. Life in all its myriad forms strives to get a jump on spring, rolling the dice to extend the growing season by a few days, soak up a little extra sunlight, take advantage of the earliest pollinators. During February warm spells anxious birds select nesting territory and sing loudly about it, both a "come hither" tune for the ladies and a warning to other males that they need to keep their distance.

Hawks and owls brave bitter winds, ice, and snow to nest during this month that seesaws back and forth between seasons. Hopefully their hatchlings will be alive and at their hungriest during the time of plenty soon to come. And the buffalo? They're mostly indifferent to the quickening pace of life. The good news for buffalo is the hint of green beginning to show at the base of last summer's bunch grasses. Buffalo understand spring on the Southern Plains well enough to know that it's wise to keep your winter coat on at least into April. Still, that green tint of tender new grass proclaims that life is good at least for the moment, and that's all that really matters here where buffalo truly do still roam.

MARCH ANEMONES. A sure sign of approaching spring: anemones flowering in one of the refuge's prairie dog towns.

March

The first week of March arrives in the refuge somewhat spring-like, but with a bit of an edge. The weather has been cool, temperatures held in check by low overcast, and the northeast wind has a bite to it, especially on the open prairie.

Elk are grazing on a flat mesa near the core of Charon's Garden Wilderness and the Crab Eyes, a pair of vertical granite columns supporting large boulders that look like softballs balanced atop the narrow ends of baseball bats. The elk, subtly beautiful in shades of chocolate and vanilla, blend perfectly with the dry grass.

Little streams tumbling down out of the uplands are trickling now, and the grass along them is green and a buffalo magnet. Trout lilies, nodding on thick stems, grow among the boulders scattered at the base of the granite outcrops, while tiny bluets and pink spring beauties add flecks of color to the bleached prairie thatch. The first bright yellow wild parsley and paler yellow puccoons are beginning to flower; the season of low growing, hairy-stemmed, cold hardy flowers are poised to attract early spring insects. Some days will be too cold for both flower and pollinators. But others will be as warm as early May, and on those days flowers, flies, bees, and bee mimics will descend like blackbirds flocking to a cornfield, ready to begin the serious business of mining pollen and serving as sex surrogates for the first wave of flowering plants.

Crab Eyes seems like a good spot to choose a boulder as big as a mini-van, settle back out of the wind and ascertain if a few low notes from a small wooden flute I've tucked into my day pack can blend into the wild ambience of the place. However, my music doesn't impress the skinny old buffalo bull lounging unseen in the tall grass on the opposite side of the boulder. The bull leaps to his feet, nimble as a startled deer, also startling the flute player in the process. After a few hops the massive animal appears to regain his composure and walk regally, albeit a bit stiffly, down to the little stream for a few nerve-reassuring mouthfuls of green grass. When I manage to hit a few high notes on the flute, the visually agitated old bruiser heads for higher ground, doing whatever necessary to bring a merciful end to the open-air talent show.

By late in the afternoon the clouds are breaking up, the weather warming and a small herd of bison cows are feeling frisky as they move across the mesa top where the early morning elk fed. The cows are headed somewhere at a trot, and they buck, joust, and attempt to mount each other in the sort of play most people don't expect from that solemn animal gracing the face of a buffalo nickel. A brown female northern harrier glides over the mesa maybe ten feet above the grass, searching for protein in the form of anything from cottontail to cotton rat. It's countdown time to the spring equinox, and life is surging, both above ground and below it.

The following week the wilderness plays host to several days in the 70s, with light southeast winds, whipped cream clouds, sprays of white flowers on wild plums, and oval green seeds not much smaller than a fingernail on the elms bordering the streams. A goatweed leafwing butterfly, an overwintering adult, zips past overhead, its flight somewhat erratic yet strong and fast. These butterflies are tough enough to withstand the cold and thus able to emerge early and engage in the serious butterfly business of finding a mate. When fully spread, the insect's upper wings are an eye-catching reddish orange. Perched and with wings folded vertically, the goatweed leafwing suddenly becomes a well-camouflaged dull, dry leaf.

The ability of overwintering insects to provide their own antifreeze seems rather miraculous, but it's a valuable trait here where winter can be harsh, but rarely for any length of time, and with rare frigid spells punctuated by balmy, spring-like periods. For some insects, surviving falling temperatures is a simple matter of producing enough glycerol to keep their cells from freezing. When the weather warms, the torpor ends, glycerol production ebbs and the bugs are back on the wing, doing insect business in some eye-catching, interesting manner.

A deer antler bearing six points serves as an ornament amid a patch of wildflowers along the trail. Shed antlers are like the health food section in the neighborhood pharmacy, vitamins and minerals made available for the prosperity and well-being of gnawing rodents. In turn the rodents provide for the health and prosperity of red-tailed hawk, western diamondback rattlesnake, coyote, fox, and others that form the many interlocking links in the food chain. Break the chain in too many places and strength erodes, and in time the system grows too weak to function as a balanced, thriving entity. Essentially, a refuge such as this one exists to save all the parts, a role that pioneer ecologist Aldo Leopold deemed critical. The health of any ecosystem hinges on biodiversity and the ability to buffer change through adaptation. The result is a biological machine that's capable of unlimited mileage, contingent upon retaining all the nuts and bolts that make it work. Interpreting the blueprint for quality land health is complex, daunting, and still in its infancy.

The life sciences continue to make revolutionary discoveries every year, all critical to the health and well-being of two-legged as well as four-legged.

The Wichitas serve as an excellent natural laboratory due to retention of many of its historic raw materials, with the entire northern half of the refuge set aside as a scientific study area. In essence the area consists of some 59,000 acres amid millions that have been plowed, channelized, subdivided, sprayed with all sorts of chemicals, the water table lowered by irrigation, and the entire macroclimate (and quite possibly the overall climate) changed by human activity. All this was done before science had an opportunity to even make a checklist of all the parts, much less determine which plants might benefit modern medicine, and which relationships between plants, animals, and an unpredictable weather region might yield knowledge that someday could salvage food production methods stricken by man-made climate change. We are, according to the Indians that once called these mountains home, no more or no less than the earth beneath our feet. It's a concept that's driven home forcefully when drought bakes the wheat and cotton fields, and clouds generated by functioning ecosystems drift elsewhere to deposit their life-sustaining rain. A system out of sync due to thoughtless manipulation doesn't bode well for life on earth, including our own.

Fortunately thoughts of climate ills tend to dissipate when leopard frogs are calling from the larger, permanent refuge pools avoided by smaller chorus frogs. The serenaders, probably either plains or southern leopard frogs, can be vocally riveting when the assembly is large. The sound, a chuckle, snore, or some combination thereof, carries well and mingles with the territorial calling of birds to ensure that early spring's keynote addresses are difficult to ignore.

Leopard frogs summon water snakes and snakes summon raptors with reptilian tastes. As always the appetites of spring are enormous, including those of both the reproductive and digestive systems. The nutritional benefits of green grass are enough to lure an extremely large bull elk out of the post oaks and onto a greening prairie dog town, the grass clipped short and maintained like a suburban lawn by elk, buffalo, longhorn cattle, and the prairie dogs themselves. Constant clipping keeps the new growth tender, nutritious and eagerly sought. Over time, repeated close clipping limits the amount of leaf surface needed for photosynthesis, thus weakening the root system and leaving the dog town open to invasion by forbs. Yet at the same time the prairie dogs continue to expand their towns' perimeters, allowing areas that were once heavily utilized to rest and recover. It's a system that for thousands of years has allowed for both plant and animal diversity, successful grazing, and the ongoing succession at the heart of a healthy grassland.

Deep within the wilderness area a huge boulder, covered with extensive splatters of bright yellow lichen, serves as a sunning perch for several turkey vultures. A turkey vulture in flight is a thing of beauty, as the eagle-sized birds catch thermal air currents that rise as sunlight intensifies and ride them in a soaring, lazily circling, flight. The refuge with its menagerie of large grazers is a great place for carrion feeders, but the sight of a half dozen vultures sunning on a giant rock, wings spread and looking like sinister angels of death, is a scene only a naturalist or morose poet could love, or maybe old Charon, the place's mythological chief caretaker.

Several longhorn cattle, one with a new calf, search for sustenance on a grama grass flat amid small boulders that look like old, angled tombstones scattered across a forgotten graveyard. The multi-colored cattle are beautiful, resourceful, and intelligent, yet seem out of place on a wildlife refuge.

Longhorns arrived here in the summer of 1927 when a pair of refuge employees grew concerned about the fate of these Texas cattle that played such a major role in the history of the West. Fearing that the animals were on the verge of extinction, the two men devised a plan to save the breed by establishing a small herd on the refuge. They drove more than 5,000 miles throughout the lower Rio Grande Valley and along the Texas Gulf Coast, inspecting some 30,000 potential longhorns for pure traits. At the end of the journey they selected 20 cows, three bulls, three steers, and four calves to be shipped to the Wichitas to form the nucleus of a registered herd.

The original longhorns were descended from the black cattle of Spain, a breed made famous by bullfighting. The first of these arrived in the New World in 1521. Over time other domestic strains, including cattle brought from the southeastern United States by immigrants relocating in Texas, blended with the Spanish breed to become the famed longhorn, immortalized by television shows like *Rawhide* and the Pulitzer Prize-winning novel, *Lonesome Dove*.

War and revolution on both sides of the Rio Grande resulted in abandoned cattle, and by the end of America's Civil War millions of longhorns roamed wild in Texas. These cattle were savvy survivors, able to subsist without care and hide out in the brush country, as secretive as deer. The tough, resilient longhorns were perfect for a new business that would help feed the increasingly industrialized northern states. Cattle rounded up in Texas were driven to railheads in Kansas and shipped to markets supplying a growing demand for beef. At the same time herds were driven beyond the Kansas rail stations to stock rangelands in states farther north.

Among the busiest of these cattle drive interstates was the Western Cattle Trail, stretching from San Antonio, Texas, to the Kansas shipping pens and sometimes on to Montana. The trail skirted the western edge of the Wichita Mountains where the range bumps up against the North Fork of the Red River. The 1870s proved to be a decade of turmoil, activity, and change in and around this old mountain range. Longhorns moved north by the thousands along the trails, buffalo were slaughtered almost to the point of extinction by hide hunters swarming over the Southern Plains, and the resident Indians were destined to watch resentfully, resist futilely, and grow resigned to the fact that irreversible change was rapidly overwhelming their way of life.

One of the participants in this drama, buffalo hunter John R. Cook, described this time of upheaval in his book *The Border and the Buffalo*. On page 157, he offers a glimpse of this time of transition in the Wichitas, when buffalo were gunned down as rapidly as the shooters could reload ammunition and the Texas drovers were pushing longhorns north to reoccupy the vacant rangeland left in the buffalos' wake.

In 1875 Cook and his fellow hunters "camped one night at the gap of the Wichita Mountains where the Great Western Cattle Trail crossed the North Fork of the Red River. I got a view of an island empire to be. I had purchased an elegant pair of long range field glasses. . . and with these I had a view that seldom falls to the lot of mankind for the variety of scenery. The great herds of buffalo were in sight from any point of view, east, west, north and south, but the heaviest, thick, dark mass was many miles to the west. Skirting the edge of the tablelands. . . northwest as far as the vision extended were to be seen the seemingly countless bison. Looking down the Otter Creek were many scattered bands of antelope, and yonder to the southwest were three big gray wolves following a limping buffalo, whose leg perhaps some hunter had broken.

"Coming down off the mountain east of me were hundreds of wild turkeys; looking back down the trail. . . could be seen a herd of 3,000 Texas cattle. . . on the way to Ogallala, Nebraska and finally destined for the Wind River country in Montana."

By mid-March pasture burning efforts conducted by refuge personnel result in spirals of gray smoke snaking up the contours of the mountains and at times clinging to the rock like fog. The smoke is several shades paler than the late evening silhouette of granite rimrock, backlit by a sky rapidly turning the same color as the flames curling through the grass. Fires simmering in the oaks suddenly erupt in a shower of red-orange sparks, and thick blue smoke settles in the lowlands like water running into a bathtub. The sun's last gasp results in an orange glow that turns the smoke the same cobalt blue of clouds draped over the horizon. It will be a warm night, and a mourning dove signals all is well. The time of the equinox is at hand.

On the 24th of the month dark clouds gather and the first violent thunderstorm of the fledgling spring pounds the Wichitas. Lightning lashes the bruised sky and thunder rolls over the granite outcrops like a drumroll at a parade. At times the rain falls heavily in wind-driven sheets, the downpour potent enough to renew streams, lakes, and manmade waterholes built by the Works Progress Administration (WPA) during the 1930s Depression.

Cooler weather under clear, high pressure skies follows the thunderstorm. Still, it's undeniably spring as the rain greens both prairie dog towns and prescribed burns, with elk, buffalo, and longhorns converging to share the nutritious salad. Greenish flower tassels and bronze-green tiny new leaves grace the post oak groves, and the neon pink of flowering redbud trees brightens the stream valleys.

Spring in the Wichitas has an ample assortment of harbingers, ranging from a swarm of reddish brown craneflies along a stream to black and white warblers foraging on a slope dotted with stunted blackjack oaks. A seasonal anthem echoes through the canyons courtesy of a canyon wren, singing its tiny heart out from atop a tall granite spire. The rust-red wren, jaunty with white breast and streaked flanks, launches into song clearly and slowly, ending each stanza with six or seven notes, each dropping in pitch from the previous proclamation.

The refuge's assortment of wildflowers is expanding. A walk into the wilderness reveals violet collinsia, a low-growing member of the figwort family. The flower is a two-toned little masterpiece of contrast, with dark purple petals opposite white ones. The first of the ground-hugging legumes are in flower, a bright purple, edible perennial commonly called ground plum. *Astragalus crassicarpus* matures into a round fruit once relished by pre-Columbus local inhabitants, people eager to stock their commissary with whatever nature made available.

Vegetation in the eastern Wichitas, including the refuge, is a mix of prairie, plains, and Cross Timbers woodland. The Cross Timbers are a strip of mostly post oak, blackjack oak, eastern red cedar, and black hickory forest stretching from Kansas into north central Texas. Regional aridity and fires set both naturally and by man has resulted in a stunted, gnarled tract of timber forming a barrier between the eastern deciduous forest and the mostly treeless Southern Plains.

Explorers on horseback in the 19th century found portions of the Cross Timbers nearly impenetrable. Author Washington Irving, who passed through the region in 1832, said in Chapter 10 of his book *A Tour on the Prairies* that the effort resulted in "vexations of flesh and spirit" as his party suffered while "struggling through forests of cast iron."

Originally the Cross Timbers covered approximately 30,000 square miles of mostly coarse, sandy soils. The land offered little in the way of agricultural potential, and as a result much of the Cross Timbers survived somewhat ecologically intact. Many of the oaks and red cedars, although rarely regal in the commonly accepted aesthetic sense, are part of old growth forest, with trees ranging from 200 to 500 years old. In essence their gnarly growth forms saved them, rendering the trees impractical for timber harvest. Researchers estimate that only around 1,390 square miles of Cross Timbers old growth remains intact.

The western edge of the Cross Timbers represents a biological crossroads. Common eastern species like tufted titmice, cardinals, and Carolina chickadees may mingle with mountain bluebirds in the winter. Gray foxes may cross paths with ringtail cats and porcupines. Annual rainfall of around 28 inches is ample to support oak-hickory forest. However, summer temperatures can be blistering and, along with periodic drought and fire, help maintain grassland and oak savannahs with scattered trees, a grassy understory, and the symmetry and appeal of a city park.

By the end of March the bleached brown tussocks of last summer's taller grasses have been invaded by the creeping green of new growth, some of the blades already five to six inches long due to protection by coarse, dry stems lingering from last summer. The plant world is growing greener, taller, and increasingly lush. Soon many of the smaller, more inconspicuous spring flowers will be shaded by taller, more colorful, kin.

A century ago the delicate spring beauties, their slender stems designed to deter nectar-robbing ants, would have provided a nutritious addition to native peoples' diets. Underground corms or tubers were gathered to add a starchy vegetable to daily fare featuring buffalo meat. White settlers were known to mash, fry, bake, boil, or eat the corms raw. The results have been compared to potatoes, chestnuts, and radishes, depending upon the keenness of one's appetite.

The anemones or "windflowers" of the refuge were once believed to flower only when the wind blew. Of course during March on the plains the wind generally does blow, and these elegant little flowers are wind-pollinated. Anemones, along with several other early spring flowers, have evolved a relationship with ants for seed distribution. Certainly the labor-intensive little insects are up to the task, and the flowers sweeten the deal by including an enticement. Each seed casing comes with a structure called an elaisome that ants love to eat. Seeds are toted to the ant den, the residents devour their treat, and the seed has an opportunity to germinate in a protected underground environment. Violets and trout lilies also bribe bugs with elaisome-bearing seeds. The trout lilies, among the first of their tribe to flower and so named because some early naturalists thought the purple blotches on their blue-green leaves resembled trout, spread from underground corms and essentially form colonies consisting of clones. The flowers dedicate as much as 60 percent of their energy to cloning and as little as 3 percent to seed production. At the same time they benefit a number of flowers yet to bloom. Trout lilies provide early spring nutrients to overwintering queen bumblebees. The queens in turn use this energy to establish colonies, lay eggs, and provide a new crop of bumblebees that will fertilize flowers for the rest of the growing season.

Soldiers from the eastern United States stationed at neighboring Fort Sill oftentimes refer to the Wichitas as a desert. And during the parched days of midsummer it must seem a desert to those accustomed to the summer greenery and steady rainfall of New England.

But while soldiers see a gunnery range laced with cactus and untold acres blackened by artillery shells, those who explore the mountains' secluded canyons on an early spring day will find leaf buds soon to unfurl on the same sugar maples tapped for sweet sap in Vermont, along with wood ferns sporting pale green fiddleheads shining in the sunlight due to a liberal coating of silver hairs. Some of the typically eastern species like sugar maple are most likely left-overs from wetter times and now cling to shady, moist enclaves in an environment that has grown much drier. Their presence serves as a reminder that the region has experienced tremendous change over millions of years as oceans rose and ebbed, mountains were born and worn down, and life adapted.

Charon's Garden ferns include shade-loving, mostly evergreen marginal wood ferns, blunt-lobed cliff ferns, the more dainty, dark-stemmed maidenhair spleenwort, leathery, rock-loving purple cliff-brake, and a lip fern that's perfectly adapted for the harsh weather here in this garden of granite. Lip ferns are among a group referred to as resurrection ferns, a name that describes them admirably. When the weather's hot and dry, lip ferns look as desiccated and lifeless as a piece of discarded paper sack. But when the rains return the ferns spring back to life, regaining the color and robust appearance of what seems to be an entirely new life. At times lip ferns appear to grow from bedrock, and it's not difficult to imagine that the plants simply die back at the first sign of stress. However the little ferns are tougher than they look, and bypass the severity of the seasons by shriveling up, staying alive, and waiting patiently for a reviving storm.

In the Wichitas the world of rocks and ferns may lie only a few shaded feet from a sun-drenched exposure more suited for cactus and stonecrop, or sedum. The sun-baked plants solve the problem of aridity by storing their own moisture, and few sights in the mountains are more lovely than an expanse of granite bedrock, soil thin to nonexistent, yet striking nevertheless due to the teacup-sized flowers of prickly pear and echinocereus cactus, the blooms a polished butter yellow and electric magenta, the lichen-streaked granite covered with a carpet of golden stonecrop with little star-shaped flowers that form a carpet where it seems nothing could grow.

Cricket frogs are in fine voice from their streamside calling stations beneath ferns reviving here at the end of March, their voices less musical than some of their amphibian kin, more like a constant clicking than anything that might resemble song. A prairie lizard, not much longer than an adult's index finger, has stationed itself on a dark and knotty persimmon tree, where it soaks up sunlight and stays on the lookout for a potential mate.

Prairie lizards tend to be climbers and prefer edge habitat, such as places where granite outcrops give way to grassland or along the margins of woodland groves. They turn a few shades darker gray in colder weather, lighter gray when it warms. This particular male is a handsome specimen with a pale yellow stripe down gray flanks and bright blue patches on throat and belly. The blue indicates the lizard is actively seeking a mate, ready to advertise his eagerness by doing "pushups" that better display the more vivid seasonal markings. Males that attain and defend the most strategic perch are more likely to be among the successful solicitors.

Bobwhite quail, the popular game bird of southern hunting legend, are still in their familiar social assembly known as coveys, evidenced by the dozen or more that flush a few yards ahead of me near the edge of a tightly intertwined patch of low-growing blackjack oaks. It's a warm day in the high 60s, the first of April less than a week away. Massive dollops of white clouds tinged with gray sail overhead like ships on a gentle south wind sea.

It's an afternoon made for buzzing insects, but the boulders near the mouth of Styx Canyon add a more menacing note. A sheltered, horseshoe-shaped opening in mostly solid granite is ringed with bedrock slabs with narrow gaps beneath their massive bulk. And that's where the western diamondback rattlesnakes have emerged from dens to sun on this south-facing slope. The snakes aren't particularly active, yet alert enough to retreat just a bit if I edge over the invisible line that marks their safety zone. There's no rattling at the moment, just snakes staring at an intruder who stares back at one of the most maligned creatures of the southwestern wilderness.

The larger snake protruding from the crevice exposes head and tail but not all of the midsection. It's a beautiful animal, a rusty reddish brown that blends well with the reddish rock, a dorsal diamond pattern edged with yellowish white, tail several inches of alternating black and white bands tipped with the infamous rattle, this particular one with 11 segments. A smaller snake appears to be about three feet long and much smaller in diameter than the larger rattler, easily as big around as an adult male's forearm. After a minute or so of this stare down the smaller snake seems to grow a bit more agitated, rattles and retreats into its snug hideaway. The larger diamondback responds with a few half-hearted rattles and retreats a few inches, but not completely out of sight.

Later in the afternoon, near the same spot and with the temperature a few degrees warmer, the hike back down the mountain reveals two more sunning western diamondbacks near the edge of a low granite ledge. This time the larger of the two snakes forsakes any pretense of sociability and begins to rattle, the buzzing accompanied by a loud spitting sound. Then both snakes head for cover.

My first encounter with denning rattlers in the Wichitas occurred one afternoon following a morning of cool rain. By three p.m. the sun had been shining for several hours and the day had warmed considerably. A friend and I were hiking on the west flank of Elk Mountain when I heard him gasp as if he'd seen a ghost.

We were crossing a large, slightly tilted granite slab devoid of vegetation. My friend was several feet behind, and when I turned he was staring at the rock and pointing down while attempting to find words lodged in his throat. It seems he'd almost stepped on a coiled and very large western diamondback, the same snake that in my inattentive serendipity I'd just stepped over.

With adrenalin adding a booster shot to our observational skills, we noticed that the slab, which could have easily accommodated a 4,000-square-feet home, was dotted with sunning rattlers that had emerged following the cool rain to soak up some prime spring sunlight. Fortunately for the pair of nitwits that had managed to infiltrate their spa due to dumb luck, the snakes were extremely torpid, and in fact paid us little mind when my hiking buddy posed repeatedly for pictures with his boot within inches of unconcerned, triangular pit viper heads.

That's the kinds of stunts twenty-somethings do to display their bravado, and I wouldn't recommend posing for closeups with the residents of a diamondback den that's out taking the spring air. It's best to admire, then retreat or go around. After all, it's their territory.

Rattlesnakes are fascinating creatures with a bad rap. Certainly they are highly venomous and their bite is deadly serious. However they aren't malevolent beings that go out of their way to sink fangs in human flesh. I've had close encounters with rattlers for over 40 years, and every snake I've encountered was on the defensive and doing its best to get away. Snakes that bite generally are snakes that are handled or stepped on. Therefore the best way to avoid rattlesnake bite is to watch where you step, keep your hands to yourself, and admire the snakes from a distance.

Spring is mating season for diamondbacks, and lengthening days find the rattlers dispersing in search of a territory replete with ample rodents. The females give birth to live young in late summer/ early autumn. Little diamondbacks are born with both fangs and venom. There's no nursery time in a rattlesnake's world—snakes that survive have to immediately get down to the business of staying alive. As days grow shorter and temperatures drop, young rattlers rendezvous with old in warm winter quarters. However contrary to rattlesnake folklore, the diamondbacks don't actually hibernate. A warm spell in the southern reaches of rattler range may find the snakes out and active. A friend of mine who owns a ranch in northwestern Oklahoma, over one hundred miles north of the Wichitas, drove one of her favorite Labrador retrievers to the veterinarian's office following a rattlesnake bite on Christmas day.

The walk out of Styx Canyon on this languid late March afternoon proceeds to the accompaniment of a wild turkey spring concert. Big toms with long, drooping beards and young jakes with smaller, spindly masculine adornment gobble and strut for the ladies while hens rummage, cluck, and gab among themselves in liquid, purling notes. Multi-colored butterflies have been riding the softly blowing south wind since mid-morning, while a drab brown dragonfly with clear wings hovers like a helicopter over a pool in the canyon. North facing, shaded canyon walls remain plastered with delicate, bright green ferns—Charon's Garden modern art. Drier slopes are festooned with grayish ferns up to 10 inches long. Rock wrens scold from the granite rim overhead, incensed over my intrusion into a cave entrance hidden behind a waterfall pouring into a natural stone bowl lined with soft green fronds.

The cave stores century-old trash: rusty barrel staves, broken glass, pieces of tin can rusted paper thin. More than a century ago a miner, enthralled by rumors of gold, came to these mountains, pick axe and dynamite in hand, ready to assault the mountains and retrieve the riches he felt he deserved. In the meantime he slept in this cave, watchful for rattlesnakes, drinking from the spring, maybe even noticing the fern fiddleheads unfurl in the spring, just as I'm doing today. If so, I can't help but wonder if the man ever stopped for a moment to relish the richness of his surroundings, or if his hunger for wealth hidden in the rock dominated his every waking thought and deed.

The "gold strike" that drew thousands to the Wichitas was a bust. Little more than a rumor at best, it exploded into a swarm of men sleeping in caves and digging horizontal holes in solid granite, like the one near this fern-shrouded spring. In a way, it seems that the miner dug his own grave here, a grave for his soul if not for a body strong enough to remove tons of rock on the strength of a rumor and little more. The pink granite he chipped away still stands in a nice little pile near the entrance, a proper headstone for a life not so well spent. And the wreath? The ferns will suffice. They drip with cool water from the rock, the real miracle of this place, more precious than any traces of gold.

April

It's April, a time of both natural and spiritual renewal in the Wichitas, and therefore a perfect time to seek seclusion in the refuge's Charon's Garden Wilderness: a rugged, exposed jumble of granite boulders, water-carved canyons, and small streams bouncing over slick stairways of small waterfalls. This morning a fierce sun illuminates a haze of heavy, humid air, a gift from the Gulf of Mexico arriving from the Texas coast. It's that time on the plains when warm south winds drape themselves over the low mountains in soft, luxuriant currents, breezes that explore the recesses in each little canyon and cling to granite outcroppings, eventually coaxing the growing season out of the rock.

Yet even now, in the season of rebirth, a chance of a late frost or even a hard freeze persists. However, native plants are generally prepared for April's weather moods and use their own adaptive chemistry to survive cold fronts that slide down from the north, slam into warm Gulf air currents and erupt into violent thunderstorms. Days following these seasonal weather confrontations oftentimes feature cold winds and bright blue, high-pressure skies.

SPRING TONIC. April rainfall cascades over granite bedrock in the southeastern corner of the refuge.

As a result, heat escapes into the atmosphere after sundown, winds tend to die down, and plants endure a few hours of occasional frost early in the morning.

Sometimes the fronts are strong enough to produce a hard freeze with several hours of nighttime temperatures well below 32 degrees Fahrenheit, a situation that can be severe enough to damage delicate oak leaves and flowers. A killing freeze in April can result in the loss of autumn's acorn crop, a hardship for wildlife species that count upon hardwood mast for autumn calories. Fortunately such truly hard freezes are a rarity. The average growing season here is April 1 to November 1, with a 90 percent chance that the final frost of the season will occur before April 11. At the same time, there's only a 10 percent chance of a frost or freeze before October 21. Therefore in April the early flowering plants keep their allegorical fingers crossed and cautiously react to longer days and shorter nights, with energy for renewal equivalent to the daily photoperiod, or length of sunlight. Already here on the fourth day of April, gum bumelia or chittamwood trees wear small lime-green leaves and fragrant sumac displays nondescript clusters of tiny yellow flowers, a tangible boast concerning their cool season hardiness.

Enough small white daisies carpet the landscape to provide an elegant backdrop for an early Easter. A search along a stream bank, especially among the stiff brown clumps of dry switchgrass, reveals the large, dark purple violets that country kids once gathered for their mothers' first bouquet of spring.

Easter Sunday appears as a popular date in my Wichita journals. It seems that most of the years I've lived near these mountains I've spent Easter in "church" here in this place containing sacred sites not only for Native Americans, but also for countless non-Indians as well. I've heard individuals ranging from local Indian artists to blue-eyed, blonde haired surgeons refer to the Wichita Mountains as their personal sacred ground. Generally it's the more majestic places, the Tetons, the Yellowstones, and the Yosemites that invigorate America's Hallmark and *National Geographic*-influenced appreciation of the natural world. Here, however, a sense of something more than meets the eye, something other than the ordinary, seems to speak to visitors ranging from youth groups, to elderly packed tightly into tour buses, to young soldiers training at adjacent Fort Sill.

Certainly part of the emotional appeal is that the wildlife refuge, with its limited development and structures dating back to WPA days, functions as an open air window to the past. This actually is the place where cowboy and Indian sagas were the mainstream, the geography where George Custer reviewed his troops and Geronimo died. It's not all that difficult to glance out across the landscape and imagine countless decades of free-roaming buffalo herds, Kiowa and Comanche tepees silhouetted against a blood-red sunset and Spanish friars carefully scrutinizing each tiny stream, certain they'll soon spot a glimmer of gold.

For centuries people native to this region climbed these summits to seek spiritual communion with their deity. Over time, Plains Indian religions were replaced by Christianity, yet a sense of the old-time sacredness still persists. In stark contrast is the annual Easter Sunrise Service held annually at a developed enclave within the refuge known as the Holy City. This passion play has been held here since 1926, on 66 acres leased from the refuge by the Wichita Mountains Easter Pageant Association.

According to the association, the 1936 event drew some 100,000 to watch 2,000 cast members chosen from among 65 towns and cities reenact the final days in the life of Jesus Christ. At one time the event received federal funding. In more recent times the American Civil Liberties Union filed suit, asking for the removal of what amounted to a religious theme park from federal land. Eventually a federal judge dismissed the case.

The pageant and park was the brainchild of Reverend Anthony Mark Wallock, who visited the refuge and felt that the terrain looked much as Israel might have looked during biblical times. Wallock, who died in 1948, worked to establish, promote, and oversee both the passion play and the construction of the Holy City, a task undertaken by the WPA in the mid-thirties. Craftsmen utilized native stone to construct exhibits including Wallock's vision of Pontius Pilate's judgment hall, Calvary's mount, and the Garden of Gethsemane. Surrounding the biblical scene are granite towers and walls. Today the site includes a chapel and gift shop.

Even today, hundreds still arrive early on Easter morning to shoo away the prairie dogs and listen to loudspeakers shatter the tranquility with a canned Easter message. It might seem more appropriate for the refuge to sponsor an Indian intertribal pow-wow, considering this actually was a holy place for native peoples at one time. However the pageant has persisted, and is now a more wholesome family event, considering that for a time during the mid- to late-1900s the event gained a reputation as a gathering where teenagers could stay out all night and drink with their parents' misguided blessings, the latter figuring an Easter pageant should be a safe enough place for young people of the opposite sex to mingle.

Partying with a capital P wasn't all that uncommon in the refuge during a period that began in the late 1960s and continued until refuge officials took measures to reduce lawless behavior. Once, in the early 1970s, while camping overnight at Sunset Lake when that area was open to overnight visitors, I watched several parties of extremely intoxicated teenagers set fire to several standing trees in an oak grove, just for the sake of enjoying a king-sized campfire.

Forty Foot Hole, a beautiful spot along West Cache Creek containing a series of waterfalls dropping into stone basin pools, was for years a well-known skinny-dipping hangout for the region's counterculture contingent, the participants content to get high and catch some of the rays the refuge offers in abundance. For a while it seemed the Wichitas were destined to become a vast playground for G.I.s, thrill-seeking kids, and religious fundamentalists until the staff cracked down by closing a number of areas to overnight access, concentrating visitors into a single, centrally located, limited access campground, and elevating the presence of trained law enforcement to control the unruly two-legged herd.

Today, as it has since 1962, average annual visitation here routinely exceeds one million, keeping the refuge at the top of the list as one of the nation's most popular. A lack of public land in north Texas makes the refuge a magnet for a booming region that includes Dallas, Fort Worth, and Wichita Falls. The popularity of the place prompted the U.S. Fish and Wildlife Service to invest in a spacious, state-of-the-art visitor center. At the same time, increased emphasis on interpretation, public relations, and law enforcement has become a must simply to keep the Wichitas from being overwhelmed by the public and losing its biological integrity as a result.

But none of this seems to matter when I'm at my own personal church in some secluded canyon, where the only reminder of the outside world is an occasional military jet flyover. Rather than Easter eggs I've managed to find snail eggs sequestered in a clear gel along with the parent snails, both beneath flat rocks in a small stream. Large mayfly nymphs that appear ready to emerge into winged adults share the same dark space with the snails. Swarms of tiny gnats dance above the stream, and just on cue a pair of blue-gray gnatcatchers appear, looking like miniature mockingbirds, vocals a quarrelsome-sounding buzzing, the birds constantly on patrol amid the new, pastel green leaves of post oak trees bordering the small stream.

At such moments it seems appropriate that Easter and Earth Day sometimes share the same month. I can't imagine any form of heartfelt human spirituality or concept of a higher power that could, or would choose to ignore the sacred uniqueness of this planet. I've always felt that the tangible wisdom underlying Genesis, the elemental facts of life that can be seen, felt, and appreciated in natural phenomena ranging from a bolt of lightning to a raindrop, are best expressed in a truly wild setting such as a wildlife refuge or wilderness area. What better spiritual testament, new or old, than the original canvas itself, a natural work of art that remains unblemished, left for the ages in a living museum where the past is also the present and always evolving, the price of admission a sense of wonder, the ceiling always open to the sky?

Charon's Garden, a small wilderness area in an unlikely place, is an Easter sermon in itself, a place that a prophet gone alone to commune would seek out and approve of. This and other minor wilderness on scattered Midwestern public lands were popular political offshoots of the growing environmental movement that inspired the original Earth Day, held in April 1970. States in the nation's midsection, where public acres are an exception rather than the rule, found it difficult to propose federal areas that would qualify for wilderness designation. One area that fit the criteria was the western end of Wichita Mountains Wildlife Refuge, which remained roadless, rugged and little changed since the time Native Americans hunted here.

When the nation's original wilderness act was passed in the 1960s, the bill's authors explained that "a wilderness, in contrast with those areas where man and his own works dominate the landscape, is hereby recognized as an area where the earth and its community of life are untrammeled by man, where man himself is a visitor who does not remain."

Writer Edward Abbey, a voice for the wilderness philosophy taking shape at the time, was more eloquent. He told Dale Volz, in an interview that appears online in "A Chat with Edward Abbey": "love of the wilderness is more than a hunger for what is always beyond reach; it is also an expression of loyalty to the earth which bore us and sustains us, the only home we shall ever know, the only paradise we ever need …."

Another of the original Earth Day voices was that of the biologist Rachel Carson, whose book *Silent Spring* was a catalyst in banning DDT, a pesticide that was decimating wildlife populations across the country. Carson pointed out that "those who contemplate the beauty of the earth find reserves of strength that will endure as long as life lasts. There is a symbolic as well as actual beauty in the migration of the birds, the ebb and flow of the tides, the folded bud ready for the spring. There is something infinitely healing in the repeated refrains of nature—the assurance that dawn comes after night, and spring after winter."

The truly poetic voices of the Wichita Mountains granite have always belonged to those who have known this landscape the best. For the Kiowa, the Comanche, and the Wichita Indians, these low mountains, streams, and oak groves weren't a refuge or a wilderness. They were just home. Few have written more eloquently of the synthesis of landscape and culture than Pulitzer Prize-winning author N. Scott Momaday. In his book *The Way to Rainy Mountain*, Momaday confirms that people and landscape can, in time, become as one, a trinity of man, land, and the spiritual relationship that binds them. It's a relationship best expressed through allegory, including one of my favorite wilderness quotes by Crowfoot, a Blackfoot Indian. He is recorded as saying "what is life? It is the flash of a firefly in the night. It is the breath of a buffalo in the wintertime. It is the little shadow which runs across the grass and loses itself in the sunset."

It is also this place where, between my feet, a coyote has pooped a sizable collection of excrement that's almost completely animal hair. In a way it seems to say "happy hunting" in the sign language of the song dog. Red-eared sliders, a common aquatic turtle in the refuge, are celebrating spring by sunning on a big boulder that's bounced and rolled off a summit and splashed to a long-ago landing in this pool. Other piles of coyote scat are replete with small rodent bones, and coal-black tadpoles scrape algae from submerged rock. All are a small but essential slice of the creation at work, the ebb and flow of a livable planet.

This particular Easter Sunday dawns behind a curtain of low gray clouds, the south wind whipping the treetops, new grass welcoming an occasional sprinkle that's blasphemy in the eyes of the Easter sunrise service crowd but textbook manna from heaven according to resident bison. By afternoon the clouds clear and, aided by a surge of sunlight, the thermometer peaks in the low sixties.

An intermittent stream flowing from the wilderness area sings its Easter praises by displaying Carolina anemones in shades of rich royal blue, the color artists routinely apply to Jesus' robe, the same as in the painting that always hung above my grandmother's kitchen table. The flowers, waving atop 12-inch stems, are taller than most others I've found here, and offer the perfect contrast for small white butterflies that complete the picture. Beyond the narrow canyon, buffalo are dining on new green grass summoned to sunlight on the blackened field of a controlled burn, their bulk contrasting the black, white, and gray Canada geese grazing near their feet.

One my favorite spring wildflowers, the diminutive blue funnel lily, flowers inconspicuously amid last year's thatch of dried grasses.

Native to grasslands in Kansas, Oklahoma, and Texas, the little flower is delicately beautiful yet low growing and oftentimes overlooked. *Androstephium coeruleum* rarely exceeds 10 inches in height and generally rises closer to four. A true member of the lily family, the flower appears above a leafless stalk and bulb. True to its common name, blue funnel lily is funnel shaped, fragrant, and flaring into six, petal-like lobes. Best of all, it's an indicator of pristine southern prairieland, a flower fit for a place where buffalo roam.

There's a new rash of birdsong greeting this warming Easter morn. The call begins with a sharp "chip" sound, then explodes into a longer, raspier "shureee." The vocalist, perched atop a slim streamside tree, flashes a yellow eye patch and overall yellowish wash. This white-eyed vireo seems small but brash, obviously emboldened by the rush of hormones prompting him to defend a nesting territory. The bird proclaims his ardor with the zeal of a Comanche warrior fighting to save his horse herd.

By the time the afternoon temperature climbs into the 70s, bumblebees are swarming over a patch of violet *collinsia* that's flowering along the stream. Rocky pools float small brown and green elm seeds, and eastern meadowlarks join the Easter heralds. However, I've been here on other early April Easters when the weather was cold, the previous week marred by spitting snow. Despite the chilly setback, tom turkeys ignored the cold and performed their best strut to entice the hens, a show-stopping courtship set against a backdrop of elk wandering out of oak timber to graze on new green grass. On several of those chilly Easters I settled back against lichen-daubed boulders, admiring a garden of stone splattered with streaks, patches, and abstract patterns of yellow, white, and pale green. At that moment I realized that the Wichitas were celebrating the season with me, even providing mountain-sized, rock-solid Easter eggs.

During the first two weeks of this particular April the weather pattern remains the same: somewhat cool, windy, overcast mornings settling into sunny afternoons. Small white mustards are bowing out of the spring picture, retreating before the taller, brighter members of the mustard family including wallflowers or *senecio*, showy flowers reflecting the increased sunlight in shades of yellow-orange. An enormous buffalo bull has claimed several hundred acres of open prairie for his own, and when he tops a small hill his topknot and horns resemble artists' renditions of Comanche fighting men riding over the horizon in their buffalo horn hats. Today the bull's chief concern seems to be a constant itch that needs continuous scratching, a task he tackles with a hind hoof that shears away winter wool ready for shedding.

Clumps of pale yellow baptisia add a touch of subtle color to the bleached grasses, the pea-like flowers of this spreading legume another bumblebee favorite. Several flat acres where the prairie levels off into a stream bottom is covered with dark green sedges growing from gummy dark brown mud. This wet meadow is in turn littered with large, white bones. A bison every bit as big as the fellow with the itch spent his last days on earth in this spot, leaving his last will and testament for the coyotes to scatter.

One chilly morning almost teases the region with frost. Under a clear sky the temperature drops into the 30s, but a light south breeze promises a quick warmup. By mid-afternoon 60-degree readings prompt the lingering twitter of field sparrows, the birds singing from multi-branched mesquite trees bearing tiny new leaves.

In Southern Plains parlance leaves on mesquites mean winter is finally history for another season. Folklore aside, they're a welcome addition to the day, along with swelling flowering buds on buttonbush along the streams, shrubs with new leaves ranging from yellow-green to rust-red. When the white, ball-shaped flowers are in bloom the butterflies will seek them out, noticeably the big swallowtails. Tiger swallowtails cruising on yellow wings etched in black are among the earliest of the big butterflies to fly, arriving in sync with the taller, showier flowers. A plum thicket sporting new green leaves has been invaded by webworms, caterpillars with a taste for plants in the rose family and engineers of tightly knit, sticky webs that help protect them from avian appetites.

In the eastern United States early spring is sometimes referred to as the mud season, but in the refuge there's minimum snowmelt to contend with. Still, spring rains suffice for enough saturated earth to allow for buffalo tracks brimming with seepage, and ample sedge meadows to become stacked high with bison fertilizer. It's recycling at its finest, with both urine and feces left in place to nurture the pantry. Beyond a rounded prairie knoll, three elk, interrupted while grazing, trot toward an oak grove less than a half of a mile away. I watch them through binoculars, and the gait seems almost comical. The horse-sized cervids carry their heads high and necks arched back, nearly in an S-curve. One of the animals, a young bull sporting a pair of short, straight antlers, seems so dingy here at the end of winter that I try to imagine him in a few weeks, shed of his winter hair and fat from all the excellent grazing now at his disposal.

Already mosquito larvae, commonly called wigglers, are jerking up and down in the rain-filled rock pools that dot the prairie. Bedraggled monarch butterflies, most likely adults that overwintered in Mexico, seek appropriate plants for egg laying. This overwintering generation is frayed and faded, ready to locate tender young milkweeds, lay eggs, and die. In a matter of weeks the next generation will hatch, eat, grow, pupate, and emerge as brilliant orange and black adults genetically programmed to continue the journey north with spring's advance. Several ensuing generations will live, reproduce, die, and follow spring as far north as the Canadian prairies. The final generation will then drift south during migration, returning to Mexico as an overwintering flock and bedazzling the autumn skies during a journey that peaks here in late September and early October.

Around the middle of the month on a warm afternoon stirred by a light south wind, a wilderness resident decides to expand its horizons. The western diamondback rattlesnake crosses the wilderness boundary, then a paved road, crawling intently toward a mix of prairie meadow and post oaks on the other side. The snake's journey takes it past dark rock that serves as a nursery for a wildflower garden of uncommon beauty—sprays of royal blue wild indigo, yellow ragwort, and redroot shrubs with white flowers. Overseeing all this floral enchantment is a collared lizard in brilliant shades of blue and gold. It's enough to make a chestnut-colored buffalo calf want to buck and snort amid undulating acres of green grass. In the distance, beyond the rattlesnake's trajectory, a dozen or so do just that.

A few cool days feel like what my mother always referred to as blackberry winter. According to her interpretation, blackberries are programmed to flower during a traditional cool spell in the spring, rather than the reality that spring in this region is a give and take of warm and cool, and odds are blackberries generally will be in flower when warm weather turns cooler, as it periodically does.

Finally, following three days of cold north breezes, the wind once again blows from the south and the temperature shoots up to 80. Spring, following a brief slowdown, is back on the fast track, and the collared lizard is back on his sunning rock, showing off breeding colors as blue as the sky.

Basking male collared lizards are slow to retreat from their basking spots, oftentimes allowing photographers excellent closeup portraits. Some, unaccustomed to these big lizards, find their size disconcerting: up to a foot long including tail, plus a large head resembling a miniature Tyrannosaurus rex. The lizards also are capable of rearing up and running on their hind legs at unnerving speed.

I've interrupted a collared lizard sunning on the bedrock banks of a stream and watched it dash away on its hind legs, crossing the stream in the process. The sight of a large lizard "walking on water" is a humbling one, especially if you tend to be superstitious. At times the lizards' propensity for running on their hind legs can result in a lesson in humility. Once, while eating lunch on the ground near an oil well, a half-dozen or so tough, grease-stained workers were taking turns tossing pebbles at a big male collared lizard basking on a rock around 30 feet away. After a few minutes the lizard seemed to decide he'd had enough torment.

Suddenly the seemingly torpid animal reared onto its hind legs and made a dash for a safer sunning spot. Unfortunately, the lizard's path headed directly for the patch of earth where the roustabouts had parked their posteriors.

Collared lizards on the run can reach speeds of up to 16 miles per hour, and this particular lizard appeared to be one of the fastest among his tribe. In a matter of seconds the animal was upon the workers and past where they'd once sat. Food cans, forks, and water jugs were either scattered across the grass or still in the air. A few ounces of upright lizard routed the men with space to spare, and some of the squeals were so high pitched it's best they went unrecorded.

A small herd of buffalo bulls lounging in and along the edges of a prairie dog town and nibbling at late April green grass have their squires with them today. Cattle egrets, small white wading birds up to around 21 inches in overall length, putter around the bulls, searching for and consuming insects drawn to the herd, and at times picking off a few parasites for brunch. Cattle egrets didn't settle in North America until 1941, arriving here after migrating to South America from Africa where they'd enjoyed a long and successful symbiotic relationship with both wild and domestic cattle. No one can say what prompted the migration, but it's been a successful move to say the least. Today cattle egrets are common across the country, where millions of cattle share ticks and biting flies with these wide-ranging winged appetites.

The season's taller, more colorful flowers have summoned a day-flying hawk or sphinx moth. Sometimes referred to as hummingbird moths due to their similar size and flight, sphinx moths are strong fliers with muscular, tapered bodies and slim wings. The insects hover like tiny helicopters and insert their long tongues into flowers with deep-throated, hard-to-get-to nectaries. Hawk moths are capable of bursts of flight reaching 30 miles per hour, and tropical species have evolved tongues as much as 10 inches long to cope with flowers that otherwise would be left untapped.

Today it seems that the dark world of the woodlands is closing in as foliage continues its explosive growth. The stream bottom fills with green shade as the canopy of mixed elm, ash, walnut, and chittamwood strives toward maturity. In the distance on the prairie the brighter green of native prairie grasses remains spotted with dark, almost black patches of sedge. It's a buffalo's vision of nirvana.

The afternoon is warm enough to cause elk to seek shade. One young bull, swelling bumps on his skull where heavy antlers resided weeks before, rests in the shade of a single red elm tree near a brook that's clear and flowing from recent rains. A larger pool upstream holds a pair of wood ducks, the drake, handsome in blended plumage featuring red, black, white, buff, and iridescent green, swims next to a drab brown hen. An adult mayfly with dappled brown wings settles onto my glasses, while ticks climb aboard from the other end. The closely clipped grass of both the prairie dog towns and acres burned by refuge personnel functions as a bison magnet. Reddish brown calves react to a beautiful spring day like kids in a park. The bucking, kicking, quick dashes, and mock battles build muscle and bone, hearts and lungs. Plus it's an excellent sideshow for newly emerged prairie dog pups that literally feel the earth move beneath their feet as the dogtown becomes a buffalo calf playground. Periodically the pups turn to their mothers and touch teeth to teeth, a "kiss" that strengthens social bonding.

Spiderworts are flowering along low granite bluffs bordering a small stream. These exotic plants look more at home in the tropics, and are among the first of the big, showy spring flowers. The dark blue or purple flowers only last a single day, yet each plant may produce 20 or more before the end of the cycle. The species flowering from this backdrop of pinkish-orange bedrock grows knee high, and when several plants are flowering at once the scene is one of wild luxuriance. Spiderworts contain a sticky sap that attaches to the finger and stretches, producing a thin strand that some say resembles a spider's web. However I've always thought that the long, stout blue-green leaves, growing from the main stem at right angles and then bending back to earth, resembled the legs of a giant spider.

A pair of spotted sandpipers, one teetering up and down like a windup toy, searches for insects along the water's edge while a buffalo bull, showing the effects of diarrhea induced by all the rich spring vegetation, strides purposefully towards a lush meadow to further his condition. Wild four o'clocks or umbrellawort are in bloom with dark, wine-colored flowers, while the inconspicuous, yellow-green flowers on slim, six-feet-tall hop trees add a lemony scent to what is already a rich spring aroma. Walking into Styx

Canyon, it's difficult not to marvel at the floral show: the bright blue little iris called blue-eyed grass, reddish orange Indian paintbrush, white prairie larkspurs, and orange globe mallows growing on six-inch-long stems.

Wild grapes are flowering, the clusters of yellowish green flowers bland in comparison to the carpet of yellow prairie flax blooming below the viney tangles. Yet it's obvious there was homicide in this floral Eden at some time during the night. Stair-stepping stone basin pools that allow spring runoff to tumble down from the lip of the canyon are littered with Strecker's chorus frog remains—a head in one pool, a torso in another, the calling cards of some predatory midnight rambler.

April on the Southern Plains abounds with migrants, including a frenetic little singer flying from perch to perch along the shrubby flank of a granite outcrop. The bird is small, maybe four and a half inches overall, but the energy and auditory carrying power seems more worthy of a species twice or even three times that size. The song is that of a black-capped vireo, and it's a jumble of twitters, trills, buzzes, and unassociated call notes, some musical, some not. Overall the song is vireo-like, but like a vireo on steroids. It's disconcerting to think that a tiny bird with so much passion for reproduction has managed to end up on the endangered species list.

Black-capped vireos migrate from the coast of Mexico to nest in Texas and Oklahoma. Their breeding range once extended into Kansas, but it's believed the birds were gone from Oklahoma's northern neighboring state by the 1930s. The vireos are hard to miss in their nesting territory, due both to their handsome markings and excitable behavior. The black "cap" fits over a strong white bar extending through the eye like the slit in a ski mask. A brownish red iris, olive back, and white breast complete the outfit for this tiny singer that seeks out brushy slopes to establish nesting territory.

These vireos require shrubby habitat, and if the trees get too big then the bird seeks new territory. Over the years clearing, absence of fire, and nest parasitism by brown-headed cowbirds have led to dwindling numbers and near extinction. Listing occurred in the late 1980s, and since that time refuge personnel have worked diligently to provide critical habitat. As a result they've managed to maintain black-capped vireo numbers at near capacity for available nesting terrain, a vital effort in the overall federal restoration program in place in both Texas and Oklahoma.

This April the thunderstorm season builds to a typical late April, early May crescendo, and it seems that this massive rockpile of mountains has sprung a million leaks. Sunlight plays upon the seepage from uncountable creases and cracks in the granite and shines bright silver in reflection. From a distance, the range appears to be a giant mirror, shattered by the storms.

Back in the heart of the wilderness, near a big cave just below the summit of the highest point, an elk skeleton, nearly intact, graces a patch of green grass between narrow rock walls that shade a pool tumbling into a miniature waterfall. Flowers grow from between the rib bones, as they do from a deer skeleton not far away. The place is so peaceful that it seems like a secluded cemetery, a place where man shouldn't linger but should at least stop for a moment and pay respects. Not far away is another cave opening, and inside the walls have been marred with spray-paint graffiti. Somehow it seems that a chapel or a memorial garden has been vandalized. In this case, the climb to the cave wasn't easy. The immortality of the vandal's ignorance required extraordinary legwork.

Near the end of the month we celebrate Earth Day. And a beautiful day it is. High pressure skies the color of a robin's egg, wind nearly nonexistent and a rarity for spring on the plains. The big prairies bordering the mountains are dotted with blue and yellow baptisia, and the buffalo wallows look like cloud shadows due to dark green sedges growing in the moisture they collect.

My walk back into the wilderness wanders through fields of wild garlic and onion, a carpet of white, violet, and purple. Sandwort growing on granite outcrops look like patches of leftover snow. A vertical granite slab, glowing orange in the bright sunlight, hosts dense sprays of dark blue spiderwort growing from cracks and creases in the otherwise solid rock. A pair of kestrels, the little "sparrow hawks" of my youth, have chosen a perch on a partly dead cedar tree along the upper edge of the cliff. They exit like tiny jets, flying sure and fast for a perch with fewer interruptions, soon to hover on the wing in wait for nourishment in the form of whatever's catchable and digestible, from a large spider to a small mouse.

Echinocereus baileyi, the little Bailey's hedgehog cactus, are flowering in what appears to be unbroken granite bedrock. The tough little cacti seem to arise from a few handfuls of actual dirt amid the rocks, flowers the size of a coffee cup, the overall plant some six-to-eight inches tall and about as big around as a man's wrist.

And, while the cactus themselves are far from showy, the flowers seem almost otherworldly in the soft April light. Perched atop the plant like a neon magenta war bonnet, they offer heavy, bright yellow pollen to insects that root within the iridescent flower rays like hogs at a trough. Nearby, in a shallow pool, a striped ribbon snake hunts at the bottom of maybe six inches of water, searching for either tadpoles or aquatic insects.

Late in the lingering warmth of the afternoon, a hummingbird winging over the prairie drops down to check out the nectar content of a wildflower. A pair of lark sparrows, perched on a basketball-sized chunk of granite, watches these aerodynamics unfold. The rubythroat checks one nectary, then another, beneath a languid sun. A blue flowering psoralea accents the shimmering green.

In the afternoon I stop to examine a post oak, a squat and spreading tree growing at the edge of the prairie. The oak has accumulated a fur coat featuring tufts of brown buffalo wool animals have rubbed off. Green stems of flowering forbs display the white froth of spittlebugs, about a teaspoon's worth of camouflage expelled by the insects so they can sequester themselves inside and sip plant sap in peace. A scissortail flycatcher, watching the world evolve from the dying crown of an aged oak, notices as an insect exits the grass and rises to its destiny. The bird is off its perch and back with a meal so quickly it's difficult to realize that the action actually happened. Flycatchers dart quickly for their meals, rattlesnakes wait patiently. And as for the buffalo bull covered with mud and taking in the bright sun, it's all part of April, a time of physical renewal highlighted by warm winds, greening grass, and long hours of contented rumination. The afternoon ends with an airborne hymn, the metallic "crank" of a great crested flycatcher that's moved into an oak grove, ready to debate the upcoming merits of May.

BISON BOYS. The thoughts of buffalo calves tend to turn to frolic in May, a month noted for temperatures in the seventies, storms, and wildflowers.

May

Most of the time May in these mini-mountains is a month of rainfall, of storms and high winds, hail and tornadoes, water sometimes descending in torrents. During May the refuge averages around five inches, a little more than two inches over the average for April and about an inch more than the average for June. By July the monthly rainfall average has dropped to some two inches while the average temperature has climbed to 95 degrees, and the pulse of the growing season slows accordingly.

Therefore May, with its ample moisture and balmy average temperature range of a high of 81 degrees, is prime for producing herbage for herbivores to eat. May is a grass-growing month, a good thing for a refuge established to nurture bison.

Some contend that averages don't mean much in a climate where the average annual rainfall of nearly 33 inches once swelled to 57 inches in 1908. . . then dipped to 15 inches two years later. The weather rule of thumb here is simple: forget all the rules. This is a region that once recorded a high temperature of 116 degrees, and once watched the thermometer drop to a low of minus 21 in what must have been a truly rugged winter.

Such schizoid weather fluctuations would seem to stamp this countryside as an impossible place to live for all but a handful of hardy lizards. But, by and large, it begins to rain in April, peaks in May, simmers during the heat of July and August then begins to rain again in the autumn. The growing season lasts some 215 days, the wind blows most of the time at around 11 mph, grass begins to green when the weather warms in April, May can seem almost tropical and spills over into a warm, humid June. Essentially it's a good climate for growing plants to feed buffalo, and the animals thrive.

It's also a good climate for growing wildflowers, and the floral display can equal many of the best in the world when the rain gods are beneficent. Dominating the May wildflower season is a member of the aster family called coreopsis. This ubiquitous species grows around knee high, blooms bright yellow, and oftentimes flowers in such masses that distant mountain slopes seem to be stained golden yellow. Few sights on the Southern Plains equal that of 50 or more dark brown buffalo cows, many accompanied by rusty red calves, grazing on bright green native grass prairie splattered with patches of golden coreopsis and red Indian paintbrush. Top it off with towering charcoal thunderheads building in the northwest above the bright rattle of birdsong, and it's easy to understand why the original people here clung to their land so tenaciously, and why visionary Americans battled to set land aside for wildlife refuges.

It's the second day of May and a recent shower has left a buffalo trail muddy enough for tracking. I've been following the prints of a big tom (male) Rio Grande wild turkey, and suddenly the author of this earthly signature bursts into view, just a few steps behind another that appears to be running for his life. The huge old gobbler in pursuit is an extremely agitated turkey, the tom on the run most likely a foolish interloper that made the mistake of soliciting the wrong guy's lady friend. The chase continues without slacking, the enraged tom gobbling with every step, the fleeing bird taking strides that would be the envy of an ostrich.

A gathering of young bull elk have wandered out of an oak grove and onto a small meadow to graze. All the elk look ragged, and several scratch at their tattered and dirty winter coats with the tips of hind hooves. All the animals in this bachelor group are careful with their developing antlers; an injury could result in aberrational growth as the headgear matures. Not far away a Canada goose hen picking at greenery near a small lake keeps her clutch of mustard yellow goslings tucked tightly against her feathered breast as she putters along, the youngsters curious yet under the control of a demanding mother.

The first of the tall penstemons are in flower. The big, bell-shaped flowers, white with violet streaks running parallel down the "throat," come equipped with a nectary designed to insure that visitors work hard for their nourishment, while at the same time doing the flower's bidding. Some in this genus are called beardtongues, and a look inside the carefully rounded and folded petals offers an explanation. The flower surrounds a special, elongated stamen called a staminode. This brushy-looking appendage protrudes nearly to the "lips" of the florescence, thus the common name.

The appendage, along with the pale purple stripes, entices insect pollinators ever deeper into the sweet spot where pollen carried from flower to flower unites with a receptive ovary to create viable seed. Different plants use different strategies, but with all it's generally an outright act of seduction. *Gaillardia suavis*, a rayless or petal-free form of the plant commonly called Indian blanket now flowering throughout the refuge, does away with the visual tapestry of its cousins and instead depends upon disk flowers to manage the job of species procreation. Rather than the eye candy of bright red and yellow petals found on its common cousin, *G. suavis* has invested in a powerful fragrance to summon the bugs for a connubial visit, thus the colloquial name, perfume balls.

This eruption of May flowering plants is a competitive one. All battle for sunlight, moisture, nutrients, and pollinators. Some seek moisture and nutrients through a highly developed root system that may compete at a different soil depth than its opponents, thus gaining a slight advantage that may result in more seeds, or maybe even more potent seeds. The process is all about reproduction, about passing along genetics that are unique to that one particular plant. Some plant species go so far as to evolve a shared reproduction strategy that serves none other than itself and a single partner. It's a daring and efficient way to ensure reproductive success—yet also one that invites vulnerability.

Yucca glauca, a plant common across the Southern Plains, has grown so specialized in its procreation endeavors that now only a single species of moth cooperates with the plant to insure the future of both. *Y. glauca*, commonly known by names including soapweed yucca, our ladies' candles, Spanish bayonet, and bear grass, is a utilitarian member of the lily family. Over centuries it has provided indigenous peoples with a source of material fiber, roots to make a soapy lather, leaves for basketry, a treatment for ails ranging from rheumatism to gonorrhea, and flower stems and flowers for hungry cattle, deer, and humans alike.

Yucca glauca's continuing success as a range plant can be attributed to a small white moth known as *Pronuba yuccasella*, or yucca moth for short. Without the yucca moth there would be no yucca. The species have evolved a relationship that's about as tightly knit as nature can make it. For openers, the yucca plant's flower structure renders it impossible to self-pollinate. Instead, the female moth enters yucca flower after yucca flower, gathering pollen as it goes, tucking the freshly gathered stash behind her head. Along the way the moth lays an egg at each succeeding flower, places it deep within the flower's ovary, then leaves a little ball of pollen on the yucca's stigma when it's time to move on.

The gift ball is a mixture of pollen gathered from any number of plants, thus providing for genetic diversity. Plus, the moth has left the ball exactly where it needs to be to insure pollination. In time the moth egg hatches, eager to feed on yucca seeds resulting from the handiwork performed by the female yucca moth. The moth's precise placement of her pollen ball results in more seeds than the newly hatched larva can eat, guaranteeing that some are left to invest in future *Yucca glauca* generations. In time the larva chews out of the seed pod, drops to the ground by a thread and burrows into the ground at the roots of the host plant, emerging as a newly formed adult moth the next time the yucca is in flower.

The relationship between yucca and yucca moth is both highly refined and highly successful, amply evidenced by the widespread nature of these adaptable, sun-loving, drought-tolerant plants. However nature, in providing a blueprint for the evolution of these two species, didn't account for the role mankind might play in their destruction. Lack of foresight or simple bad judgment, like indiscriminate pesticide use, could decimate the Pronuba population. By late in the 20th century, American agriculture was treating some 21 million grassland acres with some form of insecticide. Our growing dependence on agricultural chemicals could someday seal the fate of plants that have proven beneficial to both wildlife and people for thousands of years, especially those where a single insect species carries out the act of procreation.

The floral glory of these buffalo prairies begins to peak when purple coneflowers start to sway on May's southern breezes. Fertile ray flowers, generally pale violet, dangle from a central disk as large as a man's thumb. In time the disk flowers dry into a tough, spiny "cone" that once served as a comb for people roaming these grasslands prior to convenience stores. The ray flowers flutter on the wind like a young girl's hair, and the entire plant, growing several feet tall, graces these emerald meadows with uncommon elegance.

The stately beauty of coneflowers makes them a favorite among gardeners. In the wild these plants summon insects from butterflies to bee flies, and in great numbers. Young plants are palatable and nutritious fare for grazers, and the roots long have been an ingredient in a Native American healer's pharmaceutical pouch.

Prairie ethnobotanist Kelly Kindscher writes that various tribes used purple coneflower to treat health problems ranging from sore eyes to snakebite. The roots also served as an overall tonic and a painkiller. As a result frontier shysters were quick to seize upon the economic potential of this native curative that nature provided free of charge.

According to *The History and Folklore of North American Wildflowers* by Timothy Coffey, these ambitious and greedy entrepreneurs included Dr. H. C. F. Meyer, a patent medicine salesman working in Pawnee City, Nebraska, in 1871. Meyer learned about purple coneflower from area Indians, and began marketing a tincture of the root as Meyer's Blood Purifier. In his ads Meyer claimed "this is a powerful drug as an Alternative and Antiseptic in all tumorous and Syphilitic indications: old chronic wounds, such as fever sores, old ulcers, Carbuncles, Piles, eczema, wet or dry, can be cured quick and active . . . It will not fail in gangrene. . . In fever it is a specific. . . It relieves pain, swelling and inflammation. . . It has not and will not fail to cure Diptheria quick. . . It has cured hydrophobia."

That's a tall medicinal order for a common prairie plant to live up to, but coneflower's widespread reputation has kept it among the most popular natural tonics. The plant, marketed in health food stores as Echinacea, retains such a following that illegal root diggers have virtually eliminated the species from places it once grew in great numbers. I've personally seen native prairie hayfields, carpeted with purple coneflowers swaying in the breeze, stripped overnight.

Few of the many thousands who believe in Echinacea's curative powers take the time to consider that the plant's roots reach far beyond the shelves of health food stores. Echinacea begins with good dirt, the prairie soils assembled over the millennia by the decomposition of microbe and millipede, earthworm excrement, ashes, the breakdown of winter leaves and stems into organic material. These rich soils are the product of rot, degrading bone, urine, and excrement recycling. Components ranging from single-celled animals both dead and alive to the reeking ribcage of a rotting bull elk go into preparing a bed for purple coneflower. This expansive wildflower garden is pruned by buffalo and burned by man to keep down competition in the form of invasive woody shrubs. Spring rains provide stature, while unrestricted sunlight empowers photosynthesis. As a result the roots grow strong and deep. All these simple yet vital factors provide the "medicine" in Echinacea root. A coneflower, taken out of the native grasslands responsible for the richness of its wild chemistry, is just another ornamental growing in a pot.

I think the original inhabitants of these prairies understood that the coneflower had little medicine without the input of the world that made it. They understood that a flower, or a root, or a blade of grass was alive in the way that the air was alive, and the soil, the water, and the wind. All living things were of the earth, and thus equal in value to the sum of the whole, including man. This animistic approach to existence may seem quaint to those who worship at the altar of technology, but belief in a life force shared by all of nature, from leaf to rock to snake to coneflower swaying in the wind, is essentially a poetic expression of what modern science calls ecology. Science will tell you that a viable natural system depends upon harmony shared by closely integrated working parts for long term health and sustainability. A Kiowa or Comanche back on the old buffalo plains would have kept it much simpler. You can't pluck a flower without troubling a star, a poet has pointed out. Indigenous peoples understood the concept as the basis for universal order.

It's the fifth of May and the wind has been blowing fiercely from the south, keeping biting flies at bay from buffalo that have moved into open country to escape the winged torment that arrives with warmer weather and rain. The breeze also carries moisture from the Gulf of Mexico, and the air hangs heavy under a sun that warms the afternoon to 80 degrees. Oftentimes in spring the Jet Stream, those transcontinental winds aloft, rage overhead, carrying storms born in the Pacific or pulling down colder air from the Arctic. This morning there's enough instability in the atmosphere to fire up a storm that wrings the water out of these seasonally humid Gulf winds.

By the end of the day, six inches of rain has turned the refuge into a quagmire. At times during the storm the rain falls in blinding torrents. Even so, the grazers go on about their daily business. A band of bison bulls stolidly grazes a broad expanse of bright green prairie as if these nearly solid sheets of water are an everyday occurrence. Several cows soon join the bulls, while their calves cavort like kids playing in the spray from a broken water main.

The rain comes in irregular bursts. In between, the air remains sodden yet warm. The bright couplets of indigo buntings singing from streamside timber seems somewhat subdued by the low roar of water rushing over rocky banks. At the foot of Elk Mountain, water tumbles 30 feet into a polished catch basin, and for a while at least it could be a scene from the Colorado Rockies. However in time today's torrent will slow to a trickle. Still, it's a beautiful waterfall in a place most people wouldn't expect to find one, and the natural granite tub beneath this tumbling water has long functioned as an open air spa for visitors in need of a bath, dating back to when a hunting party first explored these low mountains, atlatl in hand, flint knapping tools bound up in a doeskin pouch.

The next day dawns clear and the temperature climbs to 80. It's a perfect day in the heart of the May growing season, on the heels of a beneficial rain that has plants drunk with photosynthesis operating on the fast track. Yesterday evening's low clouds wrapped like a turban around the serrated pinnacle of Mount Sheridan. Today it's so bright that the view from atop any one of these mountains seems to exceed infinity.

The May botanical explosion continues to expand. Antelope horns milkweed is in flower, and the plants have drawn a swarm of bumblebees. Antelope horns is named for the unique structure of the waxy, greenish yellow flowers. Nearby, thick stalks of prairie parsley are topped with bright yellow, flat-topped flower clusters with a metallic tint that sets this taller parsley apart from acres of butter-colored coreopsis.

In a few days the creeks will clear and settle into pools connected by bright riffles. For a few weeks these small, wet-season streams will resemble typical mountain streams as they rush over rocks that seem to provide the perfect habitat for trout. But by midsummer only a few, deeper pools will contain water, and tepid water at that. Still, animal tracks converging around the muddy margins of these remaining waterholes remind us that they're a vital part of this place until autumn rains break the grip of an unrelenting sun.

Ample rainfall results in ample greenery, which in turn insures a healthy insect population. This afternoon water striders are skating on the surface film of a temporary May pool. Molecular cohesion provides a "skin" or tension atop each pool, a physical bond that's capable of keeping these spiderlike scavengers afloat. Several water striders skitter in random patterns over the top of their glassy universe, casting shadows that resemble tiny paw prints. One of the aquatic insects has discovered a small dead bug floating atop the pool. In an instant it's on it like a retriever after a duck. Afterwards the water strider seems even more doglike as it darts and dodges other water striders doing their best to steal the prize. The spectacle seems familiar, like backyard mutts with a bone playing keep away from several determined canine pilferers.

The pool is as clear as an aquarium and among the rocks at the bottom a crayfish missing a pincher searches for something dead and decaying to eat. Several other crayfish, each smaller than their single-clawed senior, also prowl the interstices of their watery universe. These smaller crayfish are olive with red pinchers and tail. One however, a bit larger than average, is olive brown overall and a little more ambitious. The plain brown "crawdad" leaves the water to search among rocks above the waterline. As twilight approaches the crayfish might end up as raccoon jambalaya. For now, however, it's just a search for some unseen smorgasbord... maybe in the form of a dead frog or fish.

Crawdads, crawfish, or crayfish are actually arthropods, invertebrate (backboneless) animals with a somewhat hard yet flexible external shell called an exoskeleton. They belong to the Class *Crustacea,* arthropods that breathe with gills and come equipped with two pairs of antennae. Finally, these animals belong to the Order *Decapoda,* which includes shrimp, crabs, and lobsters. The majority of crayfish are between an inch and six inches long and probably best known for their role in Cajun cuisine. Some live in streams, some burrow in wetlands, all play a nutritious role in the natural food chain. Lobster may top the list at seafood restaurants, but I doubt that such high-priced fare is any more appreciated than a fat crayfish snared by raccoon, mink, river otter, or largemouth bass here in countless pools swollen by spring rain.

May is also for the birds. Many migrants pass through; others stay to nest and raise young here on the refuge. These enjoy a successful nesting season because spring rains have generated ample greenery to attract insects that provide nutrients for egg laying and infant rearing. Blue-gray gnatcatchers that arrived here hungry following migration a few weeks ago are now well fed and full of fight. The main issue of these first few weeks is less about gleaning insects and more about territoriality. When one intruder dares venture near a waterfall that marks the boundary of a rival, the offended bird bails from his singing perch and attacks like an inebriated bystander at a bar fight. The gnatcatchers clasp each other in midair, wings flailing, then tumble to the mud at the foot of the falls. The trespasser gets the worst of it, and soon he's back inside an invisible boundary maybe 35 yards away, still singing his lusty little heart out. At the same time the encounter has the victorious defender crooning even louder than ever, although in the case of gnatcatchers the "melody" is little more than weak, wheezy chatter.

The gnatcatcher squabble is nothing more than background noise to a yellow belly racer gliding through underbrush beneath some nearby oaks. The snake, about three feet long, greenish above and pale yellow ventrally, moves gracefully and without wasted motion. Large eyes lend themselves to exceptional vision for a reptile that's quick to eat anything from insects to other snakes, a speedster adept at capturing prey with sheer quickness. Besides, here in the breeding season racers are mostly on the move, searching for company as well as nourishment. I've always been amazed by the snakes of this tribe, by their uncanny ability to vanish from sight as if by magic. Racers remain accomplished escape artists, and thus accomplished survivors.

The birdsong din seems to abate somewhat as a big thunderhead builds to the north, looking like a king-sized helping of whipped cream stained with blackberry juice. Soon the sun will disappear behind cloud shadow and the winds will rise. But in the meantime a collared lizard, a big fellow in his bright breeding colors of turquoise and gold, catches a few lingering rays from atop a boulder at the edge of some oaks. Apparently the lizard's mind has been more on mating and less on self-survival, because an ample piece of tail is missing, probably the result of a close call with a predator or rival. Maybe the near miss will raise the "mountain boomer's" alertness level, but it's doubtful. At the moment it seems that a collared lizard honeymoon is all that matters.

The reptile remains handsome as male lizards go, even without the symmetry of a tail totally in place. Still, the big lizard isn't a tenth as colorful as the singer blurting out jumbled phrases from a nearby limb, a bird serenading the woods with bright, ringing finch-like chatter. The songster is a painted bunting, and it seems that someone has taken the small bird and dipped it in various cans of brightly colored paint. The result is a blend of hues rarely found in the natural world, especially here among the muted earth tones common to buffalo country.

Male painted buntings are among the most beautiful birds nesting in the Wichitas. From indigo blue head to raspberry belly, the bird mixes these shades plus green and yellow to produce plumage that would stand out even in the tropics, where everything from birds to tiny frogs tends to be colorful.

The sherbet colors of male painted buntings overshadow the greenish yellow females, whose job is to nest, lay eggs, and raise their young, rather than draw attention. In a way it's a survival mechanism, as with the boldly patterned milkweed bugs on a nearby clump of antelope horns milkweed. The brashly orange and black bugs wear their colors as a warning. Like monarch butterflies, the colors tell predators that as nymphs the bugs fed on milkweed plants, and as a result the orange and black markings mean a milkweed bug meal would be both distasteful and nauseating. The male painted bunting with his bright colors proclaims that he deserves all the attention while the overlooked female attends to more serious business. Milkweed bugs depend upon their unmistakable pattern to announce, eat me if you dare. Most predators have discovered they do not.

May is a month that many serious hikers prefer to seek out the stark canyons and boulder rivers of Charon's Garden wilderness, a roadless tract on the west end of the refuge. Streams are running, flowers are blooming, and the afternoon high temperatures generally remain in the low 80s, a tolerable temperature for rock scrambling and boulder hopping. This particular morning has been cloud free and bright along the western border fenceline, and by mid-afternoon the temperature will reach 85. Several warm days in a row have resulted in insects in abundance, and paralleling the upsurge in insects has been additional activity by insect eaters. Mississippi kites are back, following their winter retreat to South America. This medium-sized, handsome gray and white hawk looks fierce, and definitely acts fierce when nests need defending. But basically it's an insect eater, even though the bird has been known to clear golf courses when unsuspecting duffers wander too near a nest.

Rough-winged swallows are eagerly gleaning insects rising from a pool in Styx Canyon, their swooping, darting flight as hard to follow as a ping pong ball batted back and forth between a pair of pros. Even so, they can't compete with the ultimate insect predators, the common whitetail dragonflies with their ivory abdomens and clear wings sporting black bars. One of these handsome insects perches on the tip of a buttonbush branch, large compound eyes scanning for the slightest movement. When a midge flies near, the dragonfly is airborne and on its prey like a jet fighter pilot focused on a blip on a radar screen, except that in this case the insect maneuvers more like a helicopter and the midges haven't a chance.

Kingbirds, recent arrivals from Central America, are extremely active and feasting on insect bounty, and watching their aerial displays is like getting reacquainted with old friends. Both eastern and western kingbirds use the refuge, here where contrasting habitats converge. When I was a kid growing up on the prairie, the eastern kingbird was my favorite due to its sheer audacity. It seemed the flycatcher never wasted an opportunity to harass a bird much larger and more dangerous than itself, and I admired the natty black and white plumage and graceful, darting flight. Now, after living in the territory of both eastern and western varieties, it's hard not to love the entire tribe.

Western kingbirds are outfitted in more subtle plumage as befits their grassland range, but the mix of gray, brown, yellow, and black is beautiful in its own right. Eastern kingbirds look like they're dressed for a party in the halls of Congress. Westerns appear to be headed to the beach. Both are accomplished bug snatchers, and today a western kingbird has taken a stand in a dead elm tree. From this barren perch the bird waits until a morsel flies within range. Then, like the dragonfly on the buttonbush, the predatory flight is quick and short, the aim generally on target.

While May arrivals from Central and South America are settling in, resident songbirds are watching their first hatch, initiated back in March, graduate from flight school while still demanding a meal from mom and pop. Eastern bluebirds can't match the flying skills of aerial specialists like flycatchers, and therefore subsist on a broader diet. Still, May with its bug overload, coincides with nestlings in need of protein, and today a bluebird is scouring an oak grove, acquiescing to the demands of a young bird that's left the nest to follow the parent impatiently and loudly, still expecting constant parental input when it comes time for chow.

The young bluebird is awkward yet persistent and trails along through the limbs, obviously content to be fed and insistent that feeding time arrived some time ago. Within minutes the adult male has a bug to help sate the clamoring appetite, which it feeds to the youngster as if the little beggar was still in pinfeathers. They proceed on in this manner, the parent bird searching each leaf and limb diligently, the young bird nagging without remorse. Below the trees the path is littered with buffalo wool, spelling relief for bison that seem to be constantly scratching, rubbing, and rolling, also providing nesting material for birds willing to use everything from snake skins to highway trash when preparing a nursery for their young.

A robust clump of eastern gamagrass, flowering in the damp, dark earth along a streambed, looks more like something that would have evolved with parrots and monkeys chattering overhead rather than a favorite item on a bison's spring menu. The foliage of this native species is extremely lush, more like the exotic Johnson grass, except that native gamagrass doesn't produce the toxins that result in miserably sick cattle under certain conditions and during certain times of the year.

Gamagrass leaves flare out from the base of this bunchgrass like water from a fountain, and the stout stem is an excellent reminder that the plant is a wild cousin to domesticated corn. One botanist refers to eastern gamagrass as the "queen of the grasses" and points out that it can grow in saturated earth yet tolerates drought, contains as much protein as domesticated alfalfa, flowers earlier than other warm season grasses, produces seeds that can be ground into a nutritious meal for both cattle and for the table, and the entire plant can be chopped up for silage. This newly discovered "wonder grass" was a prairie mainstay back in the buffalo days, but declined when the prairie came under cultivation and cattle overgrazed what was left. Now that it's been rediscovered, gamagrass is the focus of research universities working to unlock the plant's genetic potential to provide for both livestock and man.

If the Wichitas have a May anthem, it's the descending trill of a canyon wren singing over the frothy cadence of a spring waterfall. It's the voice of spring in these low mountains, riveting with reproductive energy and clamorous compared to the slurred and subdued two-note utterance of a phoebe, a bird that's singing nearby. In an instant the phoebe dives off a branch overhanging a brook to snare a small white moth, then quickly perches in the same spot to sing again. The phoebe's thoughts appear to be equally split between defending its limb and snagging anything edible that flies within range of it. The canyon wren, on the other hand, sounds as if it is laying claim to entire mountains.

Beneath the phoebe a coachwhip snake, a little over three feet long, has been prowling around the rocks at the edge of the stream, probably sensing that the balmy afternoon would lead to lots of small frogs basking in the sunshine. The snake is the paler western variety, light tan with brown and reddish tan markings. The scales of the tail make it appear plaited, like a braided leather whip, thus the common name.

Coachwhips can move quickly for their size, yet sometimes prefer to freeze in place rather than flee when disturbed, a reaction that unnerves some who fear snakes and misread a natural instinct to remain motionless as an act of aggression. These snakes aren't equipped with venom and are harmless except for a tendency to bite if roughly or carelessly handled. This particular afternoon has graciously provided exceptional weather for a beautiful snake to go grocery shopping. My guess is that it will be in the process of swallowing an amphibian tidbit within the hour.

Pecan trees are flowering on a flat bench beside the stream, with dangling, yellow-green male flowers like knotted strings, ready to supply pollen to the spring winds and fertilize the inconspicuous female flowers that swell into one of nature's most perfect foods—just ask the resident fox squirrels that must be salivating at the thought of November's bounty. Food is also on the agenda of a pair of small dung beetles, but in their case it's food for eggs that will hatch into industrious dung beetles-to-be, each born with a ravenous appetite.

Therefore the parent "tumblebugs" have gathered excrement of just the right vintage, patted and rolled it into a ball, and are now about the business of pushing their treasure to a hole they've dug where fresh dung and egg will be sequestered until junior can survive above ground and make his or her own dung sculpture to go.

Rolling a ball of poop bigger than both pushers is no easy task, but dung beetles take to labor like roughnecks in need of a Saturday night paycheck. Today's ball is approximately the size of a marble, but the beetles themselves are members of one of the smaller species. Fortunately dung beetles work together better than most. This afternoon they're shoving in tandem and the progress is brisk. . . until they encounter a chunk of sand as big as the ball they're rolling. At that point one of the beetles rushes ahead, shoves the obstruction out of the trail they've chosen, then returns to work. I immediately think, way to go, guy, but then who knows if chivalry is a byproduct of gender among dung beetles? Most likely an obvious willingness to work among tribal members has little to do with gender and more to do with a shared workaholic genetic traits.

When it comes to dung the refuge is a bountiful place. Dung beetles here not only have some serious amounts to select from, but vintage varieties as well. Wichita Mountains tumblebugs don't have to settle for common cattle dung, as is the case of their cousins throughout the West. Here at the refuge, dung beetles have the opportunity to roll the real deal, the buffalo dung they evolved with and most likely acquired a taste for. Therefore, one might deduce that, to a tumblebug, a pad of buffalo plop would be the equivalent of a wine that's been aging since the days of Geronimo. Cow patties, on the other hand, easily could be little more than Ripple.

There's a place in the refuge that's a perfect May hangout for an aging buffalo bull to mull over a life of fighting, breeding, and masticating good grass, and preparing for the day when coyotes, maggots, and crows will compete for what's left of him. A semipermanent stream rolls off a mountain flank into an open, grassy valley. And, when the stream dries up in midsummer, a manmade pond nearby holds ample water throughout the year.

The valley contains deep soil and good grass. There aren't as many exposed rocks to stumble over. All in all, it's a good place to settle down in the shelter of a plum thicket and prepare to die.

This morning the old bull that's staked out his hospice retreat here in the valley lies facing the wind, buttocks as thin and angular as an old frontiersman's plow, his thick topknot blowing straight back like an old man's comb over. It's warm, and has been for several days, but the old guy has yet to shed any of his winter coat, a sign of infirmity.

After a few minutes of watching me watch him, the aging bison tries to reach his feet, but stumbles. He tries again, only to drop back to his knees. After the sixth attempt the decrepit old bull manages to keep his feet, legs splayed like a young calf rising for the first time. Later in the afternoon I find him stretched out on his side at the same spot, soaking up the warmth of the sun. At such a moment you almost wish for wolves, so that the end would be quicker and more merciful.

A dull olive yellow and absorbed by nesting duty, a female summer tanager takes a momentary time out from atop the trunk of a dead cedar tree to watch the old buffalo's life struggles. She's gathered a bill full of dried grass for a nest, and it stands to reason that somewhere nearby her mate, feathers the color of red trumpet vine flowers, has staked out a homestead amid a tall and shady post oak grove. It's been a cool morning, cloudy and in the fifties, but the steady increase in bird numbers hasn't seemed to slow. A burrowing owl stands sentinel atop a cone of dirt in a nearby prairie dog town, the owl almost clownish looking—sort of what a comic book illustrator might create to represent the real thing. Threadleaf thelesperma, a short yellow flower common throughout the refuge, forms a yellow carpet over the closely cropped, bright green dog town, and four buffalo bulls arrive for their morning repast, winter coats hanging in patchy tatters, the cool morning perfect for some preemptory head butting, pushing, and shoving before the real battles begin in earnest later in the summer.

In the distance the flanks of the granite outcrops are yellow from extensive colonies of flowering coreopsis and thelesperma. At the same time the early spring plants so eagerly awaited by grazers just weeks before have turned brown and gone heavy with seed. An introduced annual brome grass, an invasive pest in native grass pastures, droops under the weight of pinkish seeds that grow browner day by day. Sedges that added a green tint to early spring wetlands are heavy with ripening seeds, while many of the late March and April flowers, those flecks of color in otherwise bleached brown meadows, have completed the process of renewal and replenishment, and now rest in dormancy until another winter begins to wane.

May nesters have more to fear than raiding squirrels and bluejays, hailstorms and tornadoes. A brown-headed cowbird, perched atop an oak tree overlooking a white field of wild onions recently gone to seed, sings liquid, purling notes that are beautiful yet rarely appreciated by the many bird fanciers that view the singer with disgust. This male cowbird is definitely in the mood for companionship, but thoughts of territory are of little importance to this winged vagabond.

Cowbirds might be more appropriately named buffalo birds, for these blackbird kin evolved with the great herds that once covered North American grasslands. Bison attract both winged insects and parasites, which in turn fed multitudes of cowbirds. However the herds were always on the move. Therefore cowbirds became nest parasites, laying their eggs in whatever available nest they could find and then continuing on with their food source, leaving the unwary nest host to hatch and feed their young.

It was an effective strategy although not one that appealed to civilized sensibilities, especially after homesteaders arrived with their axes, plows, and cows. Land clearing and the introduction of domestic cattle opened up millions of acres to cowbirds, as well as an increased number of species gullible enough to raise large and greedy cowbird young at the expense of their own nestlings.

For cowbirds nest parasitism meant survival of the species. For bird lovers given to anthropomorphism, it was a travesty. Sweet little eastern woodland songbirds soon were rearing big, ugly cowbird nestlings, and working overtime to do it. And, in some cases, native species requiring specialized habitat needs watched as their numbers diminished due to both too many people and too many cowbirds. When it came time to assess blame, the bulk of contempt was reserved for the "callous" cowbirds.

The Wichitas' black-capped vireo is among the species that has suffered from both habitat destruction and cowbird parasitism. And, since we're not making any more land these days, protection of the vireo, an endangered species, has required the elimination of a number of cowbirds. Sadly the cowbird, an amicable singer and somewhat handsome in somber brown and black, has become a victim of its own history. Life on the move with the buffalo must have been marvelous. Life with domestic cattle and as the bane of countless bird watchers isn't quite as glamorous, especially when you're only doing what comes naturally.

By mid-month there are places where the new shoots of little bluestem grass, protected by the dry leaves and stalks left over from the previous summer, have grown as much as a foot. However that's rarely the case where the leaves are accessible. Mostly the leaves and tender new shoots race to survive the appetites of longhorn cattle and buffalo. In some spots the grazers win. In others the grass makes sufficient headway to produce tough, less palatable stems, increase the silica content that serves as an impediment to herbivores, and with good fortune grows to became a mature plant that flowers in late summer and gleams with silver seeds over pinkish leaves and stems in late autumn. These mature tussocks will serve as cover for ground-nesting birds the following spring. Closely grazed areas help create the patchwork mosaic of tall, medium, and cropped cover that's a trademark of bison range and premium habitat for many types of wildlife.

The gravel bottomed stream pools back in the Charon's Garden Wilderness where I found mating Strecker's chorus frogs early in the spring now swarm with tadpoles, many with tiny limbs and tails with prominent fins. Small green grasshopper nymphs are common in the grassy meadows bordering the stream, where the bright neon pink of flowering sensitive briar adds artistic drama to the muted gray, yellow, and green lichens covering the granite outcrops. Dragonflies are common now, and a long-horned grasshopper has indulged in a feast featuring the heavy yellow pollen of a flowering prickly pear cactus. A ruby-throated hummingbird tends to sip more daintily at the nectar provided by a white larkspur, while five rock wrens, probably quarrelsome juveniles, raise a ruckus from atop an automobile-sized boulder.

At the moment I'm not the only one taking note of the life surge that's enveloped a refuge now in throes of mating, pollinating, spawning, and sowing seed. A pair of coyotes survey the prairie from behind a dog town where buffalo calves play and their mothers take dust baths. Both of the song dogs, most likely a mated pair, appear to be in robust health, a sign that spring has been good to both the adult coyotes and most likely to a den of pups somewhere nearby.

After a few minutes of intent study, the coyotes trot on towards a grove of timber, ears up and interpreting every sound, noses investigating every nuance carried on the wind. I learned to respect coyote intelligence early, from experience while growing up on prairie ranchland. I also learned firsthand of the intense hatred many country people feel towards this little wild canine. Certainly coyotes are predators, but not the savage stock killers they've been labeled. After the native wolves were shot and poisoned into oblivion, coyotes inherited the reputation of their larger, stronger cousins. Even today westerners run hounds after coyotes on sorties they call "wolf hunts," even though coyotes can't compete with the predatory efficiency of wolves.

Coyotes are capable of capturing their own food if the prey is weak and small, but remain just as interested in carrion, wild fruits, essentially anything edible. Research on the refuge has, for example, shown that coyotes prey on whitetail deer fawns, while an adult whitetail would have to be very sick or injured to invite an attack from these animals that shrink from encounters that risk injury. Cotton rats and voles are more song dog speed, and if they tackle an adult deer, most likely it's an already ripe carcass.

Superior intelligence and cosmopolitan dietary habits have made the coyote a survivor. Some jest that coyotes and cockroaches will eventually inherit the world, and if you have any understanding of coyote habits, then it's clear that the claim is closer to the truth than most care to imagine. And, while those of us of European extraction find it easy to revile this fascinating animal, Native Americans always have appreciated the coyote's adaptability, cunning, perseverance, survivability and, at times, downright goofiness. Coyotes figured prominently into tribal folklore. A Comanche Indian friend once told me that his grandparents, whose original land allotment was near Mount Scott, would leave food out for coyotes in winter. In return, he said, the coyotes would stay for a while to gossip, filling them in on all the latest news.

Kiowa poet and novelist N. Scott Momaday explained the relationship like this, in his book *House Made of Dawn*: "Coyotes have the gift of seldom being seen; they keep to the edge of vision and beyond, loping in and out of cover on the plains and highlands. And at night, when the whole world belongs to them, they parley at the river with the dogs, their higher, sharper voices full of authority and rebuke. They are an old council of clowns, and they are listened to."

Maybe coyotes, like modern comedians of the two-legged variety, salt their communications with ageless wisdom and truths, figuring a clownish delivery makes the message more palatable. My guess is that once long ago when Jesus wandered in the wilderness, there was a coyote or some Middle Eastern cousin of the coyote waiting to explain the ways of the world, and the coyotes' role in it. According to legend the trickster sees all, knows all, yet oftentimes makes a shambles of everyday life due to insatiable curiosity. Still, coyotes take care of coyote tomorrows extremely well, expanding territory, adapting to both city and farm. I'm not so certain about cockroaches, but a world mostly populated by coyotes would tend to be a magical place, although a gossipy one, and noisy beyond belief.

By the time the middle of May rolls around, a granite bench near the edge of Elk Mountain is a showcase of flowering cactus, the big, bright flowers drawing yellow and brown beetles covered with coarse yellow pollen. These soldier beetles mine the flower's treasures like attendants at a Roman orgy, and the flower literally throbs with activity.

The prairies burned by refuge personnel in March are now vast fields of green flecked with flowers. Several bull bison alternate grazing with periodic rolls in shallow wallows amid all this green, their remaining winter hair hanging like tattered rags. A herd of buffalo cows with their calves in tow have retired to a prairie dog town for their own afternoon roll, some of the cows dropping to their front knees in an attempt to rub away loose head and neck hair on mounds of dirt surrounding prairie dog burrows. Others paw the mounds to loosen up the compact soil, then drop all the way down to roll on their backs, kicking up little clouds of dust with their efforts.

When the cows are finished, the chestnut red calves make not-so-serious efforts to emulate their elders. When they tire of attempting to learn this dust bath business they take a time out to nurse, try to learn to graze or kick, buck and butt each other on this, their very own prairie dog town playground.

Late in May I see my first roadrunner of the year disappear into an oak grove where the most striking of the early summer flowers is growing abundantly noticeable. Standing cypress, a tall, bright scarlet wildflower with a number of blossoms along a stout main stem, begins to bloom in the hot, muggy days of late May and early June. The little streams run more slowly now, and the water clarity reveals the circular nests at the bottom of the bigger pools, places where male members of the sunfish family have swept away silt so that eggs laid and fertilized won't suffer from oxygen deprivation.

The same oak grove that hid the roadrunner also shelters a member of the nightjar family, most likely a chuck will's widow. The birds are almost bat-like when they flush from beneath the oaks, their cryptic blend of brown and tan feathers a perfect camouflage. A steep, vertical granite face behind the oaks has yellow spiny asters, a flower that seems to prefer growing from narrow rock ledges and a plant that will be a flowering mainstay throughout the rest of the summer and deep into autumn. When a lark sparrow flushes I'm able to locate a nest tucked away in a little bluestem tussock, the aged grass bleached almost white and surrounded by the blue-green of new growth.

Caterpillars have consumed much of the foliage on several oak groves, and the tiny new pale green leaves replacing those lost to the infestation seem to be out of time and place, leftover from early spring. Small green nuts are now evident on streamside black walnuts and buckeyes. A bobcat strolls out of the timber and into sultry air that promises a storm.

A yellow-billed cuckoo, cousin to the roadrunner and oftentimes referred to as a rain crow by country folk, is calling on the wing when the rain comes. The cuckoo will feast on the caterpillars defoliating the oaks, and those who indulge in superstition will insist that it was the bird that summoned this late May storm.

The month ends much as it began, with rain falling in blinding sheets. This time a small herd of buffalo dash at full speed for an oak grove and the protection it offers. Others just hunker down in the taller grass, waiting out the weather as their ancestors have for more than ten thousand years. Several cow elk continue to graze on a meadow made bright green by spring burning. The color of the grass seems electrified by the ominous, stormy light, the glow contrasting paler clumps of wild alfalfa. Two bull elk rest on the ground near the cows, one topped by a very large set of antlers wrapped in velvet, the other, although a large and healthy animal, spindly in comparison due to his forkless antlers, the solitary spikes an indicator of the bull's youth.

When sunlight returns following the rain, prairie dogs emerge and look around to assess any damage. Soon the pups are once again wrestling with each other and attempting to play with their mother when a sibling isn't available. The female is indulgent with her young, a testimonial to the strong social bond that unites these animals. The pups play, tug at their mothers, then stop to "kiss," a habit that endears them to tourists and provides a means of olfactory identification.

Down by the creek a pair of green herons land in a dead tree overlooking a pool just below a newly fashioned beaver dam. Turkey vultures spread their wings to dry before taking flight, and a flock of resident Canada geese arrive to graze on the prairie dog town. In the distance a huge buffalo bull, a patriarch animal in his prime, surveys his domain from an emerald patch of prairie. The bull, a dark chocolate brown, his hide sleek following shedding, is at rest amid a patch of wild blue indigo. The lovely, multiflowered baptisia says to the world that this remains a verdant pasture of plenty. The expanse of grassland, still dripping from the thunderstorm and backed by a rainbow arching over distant mountains, is about as native as it gets, with roots reaching back to the time of famed Comanche chief Quanah Parker. The buffalo confides that May is counting down its final hours now, and that June is set to arrive lush, green, and a little on the hot side, still perfect for growing grass. . . but only if the rain gods look upon the landscape favorably.

TOGETHERNESS. Prairie dog pups ramble in search of June greenery as the weather heats up and the rains begin to subside.

June

If the rains have been generous, June in the Wichitas is generally a time of plenty. Each day the sun hangs over the land a little bit longer, edging towards the Summer Solstice, the longest day of the year arriving around June 21. Wild fruits borne on April and May flowers are ripening, grasses are growing lush and small herds of buffalo cows graze to provide nourishment for the orange-colored calves at their flanks. It's a serene scene, yet one that does little to calm the bulls. They are edgy now, shunning the communal comfort of bachelor groups, ready to test the air for the scent of cows in estrus. The lumbering animals paw and roll in prairie dog towns, but the rightful tenants ignore their massive buffalo presence and continue to mimic activity you'd expect to see on a school playground. Prairie dog pups are as energetic as kittens on a country porch, scrambling, wrestling, and interacting in ways that teach prairie dog etiquette and communication. Soon midsummer heat will dominate, and life on the refuge will turn nocturnal. But for now, prairie dog pups and buffalo calves think of little other than the sheer joy of a lazy June morning, while their mothers watch life-giving thunderheads build on the horizon and lash the mountains with lightning and thunder.

In many ways, other than sheer magnitude, the scene hasn't changed much since a June day in 1852, when Captain Randolph B.

Marcy commanded the 5th Infantry on a march up the Red River. Marcy was on a mission to explore the river to its source, and a report of his adventure was published under the title, *Exploration of the Red River of Louisiana.* The origin of the Red, now the dividing line between Texas and Oklahoma, was still a mystery at the time.

Marcy passed near the Wichita Mountains and, on the plains to the west, made this notation in his diary: "Our road during the whole day has passed through a continuous dog town, and we were often obliged to turn out of our course to avoid the little mounds around their burrows." Marcy added that the vast colony's yipping and barking sounded like the busy hum of a city. He estimated the size of the prairie dog colony at approximately 625 square miles.

Along with ample numbers of prairie dogs, Marcy encountered buffalo, antelope, several cougars, and rattlesnakes seeking to convert tender young prairie dog into prime filet. Marcy's reports concerning the massive numbers of prairie dogs and the sizes of their colonies come to mind as I, along with a half-dozen tourists, watch the antics of refuge prairie dogs so fat they seem filled with helium. Dozens of pups in a roadside dogtown attempt to coax adults into play, generally with little success. So, rather than go back to rough and tumble, the young resign themselves to accepting grooming from their superiors, along with an occasional "kiss."

Black-tailed prairie dogs are social ground squirrels weighing around one to three pounds at maturity. They average some 14–17 inches in length, with about a fifth of that dimension contained in tail. Of the five different species, black-tailed are the ones common to the Great Plains.

Prairie dogs are mostly known for—and condemned for—their diet of grass. Accused of eating grass that would otherwise fatten cattle, these once ubiquitous creatures have been shot and poisoned relentlessly since the time the buffalo disappeared and domestic cattle replaced them on native grasslands. Eradication efforts have reduced prairie dog numbers by an estimated 98 percent.

Actually, prairie dogs are omnivorous, and, along with grass, roots, and forbs, will dine on cactus, insects, cattle and/or bison dung—even each other if need be. However the mainstay of any healthy prairie dog diet remains the grass they're castigated for eating. Recently some range management experts have come to believe that closely cropped prairie dog towns can at times, and under certain conditions, actually improve livestock grazing rather than destroy it. Unfortunately for beleaguered prairie dogs, selling the concept to cattle growers has been near to impossible.

Prairie dogs like these in the dog towns that still dot the wildlife refuge evolved to thrive under the boom and bust conditions of the grasslands. They eat and store fat when conditions are good, then live on stored fat when they aren't. Standing water isn't a requirement, since the animals are able to metabolize moisture from what they eat.

Here on the refuge, prairie dog towns act as tables set with tender green salad for grazers including buffalo, elk, and longhorn cattle. On this particular morning around a dozen elk munch grass along the dog town perimeter, drawn to the closely cropped greenery that's succulent, nutrient rich, and easy to digest. The prairie dogs maintain a mowed lawn for their own safety's sake, clipping the taller grasses to improve the view. Shorter grasses allow for better vision, which in turn allows the prairie dogs to maintain a vigil for those that would convert them into protein, predators ranging from coyotes to rattlesnakes.

Below each dog town is an extensive subterranean world of burrows that provide escape from predators and the elements, along with storage and birthing chambers. Individual burrows can be as much as 100 feet long and 16 feet deep in these dog towns that thrive under the protection of state and federal wildlife agencies.

Prairie dogs on private land haven't fared so well. It's been estimated that late 19th-century Oklahoma may have contained as many as 950,000 acres of dog towns. By the late 1990s the number was a mere 8,500 acres, a 99 percent reduction. The overall prairie dog population throughout the plains was estimated to have been 200 million prior to cattle and fences. That adds up to some 400 million prairie dog pounds, at an average weight of two pounds apiece. At the same time the grasslands hosted an estimated 30 billion pounds of buffalo on the hoof. Obviously, these two animals played a major role in the ecology of the pre-settlement prairie.

The original Southern Plains grassland in its native state contained extensive dog towns averaging around four prairie dogs per acre. The animals' relationship with the land was, in the words of biologists who study prairie dog ecology, unique enough to classify them as a keystone species, or one that has a disproportionate relationship with the plants and animals they've evolved with.

Even a small amount of time spent watching prairie dog towns within the refuge reveals an obvious beneficial relationship shared by prairie dogs and hoofed grazers. Dog towns also provide burrows utilized by snakes, amphibians, burrowing owls, and the superbly adapted prairie dog predator now on the endangered species list, the black-footed ferret.

Mountain plovers nest on dog towns. Ferruginous hawks circle overhead, seeking a prairie dog buffet. The towns and their subterranean complex host unique life forms ranging from protozoa to arachnids. Therefore it shouldn't be surprising that when the dog towns were destroyed, grassland species numbers suddenly plummeted. By the early 21st century many grassland birds were in sharp decline, with several on the cusp of endangered species status.

Fortunately we have refuges like this one in the Wichita Mountains where buffalo and prairie dogs still share turf, each natural area a mecca for graduate students seeking to explore that which almost became unexplorable. Unfortunately both bison and the prairie dogs disappeared so rapidly from the West's wide open yet unprotected spaces that it's difficult for these same biologists to grasp the unique wild relationships that existed on what was once such a grandiose scale, one that was much more species rich when dog towns covered massive numbers of square miles, rather than a few square meters. There's no way to replicate the vastness of those once flourishing natural systems, nor the infinite number of microhabitats within the system. Today's scientists must depend on historical accounts, an active imagination and computer models to envision the richness of life that was once our great and grassy plains.

Modern researchers try to comprehend what may have been "normal" on the plains by comparing what's left to the only surviving grassland with much of its biodiversity remaining, namely the African Serengeti. Today's travelers crossing the American prairies mostly see a vast emptiness with a few scattered cattle and dismiss the area as lifeless, dreary, and unattractive. They fail to realize that the majority of the native ingredients are missing—the dog towns stretching from horizon to horizon, the buffalo, elk, and pronghorn antelope feeding among the prairie dogs, the packs of wolves following the buffalo, the coyotes waiting for the wolves to make a kill so they can glean a few of the morsels left behind.

Before the cow and the plow, swift foxes would have followed scent trails a safe distance beyond the coyotes, while hawks and golden eagles circled overhead, waiting for a young prairie dog to roam too far from safety. A traveler might have seen bighorn sheep silhouetted against the sky atop a bluff overlooking a prairie river, while black bears and maybe even an occasional grizzly sauntered through the cottonwood gallery forest below. Prairie chickens danced the spring away while frogs and toads called from, and mated in, ephemeral pools that were buffalo wallows during the dry season. Protected landscapes like these in the Wichitas allow visitors a glimpse of historical grassland still in good health. In fact, with the aid of a little imagination they sense that this region once *was* the American Serengeti, a land of variety, of four distinct seasons, an aboriginal culture that managed to fit in with the ecological ebb and flow, and weather sometimes so brutal that the surviving species were among the most resilient in the world, thanks to that hard-edged paring knife known as evolution.

In the late 19th century some field naturalists short on scientific training calculated that 256 prairie dogs ate as much grass as a single cow. Over time this estimate became gospel in the minds of stockmen whose financial welfare was tied to grass. Today's research weighs more in favor of prairie dogs by pointing out an adult bovine eats around 30 pounds of dry forage daily while a prairie dog consumes around 25 pounds of dry grass annually, a fraction of the original estimates. Even so, the prairie dog can't seem to shake a reputation that's largely undeserved, and as recently as 2012 still faced extermination by statutory decree in some states, sport shooting, and even federally subsidized poisoning. Conservation organizations continue to sue in behalf of this keystone species, but old prejudices die hard in cattle country.

Even though it's oftentimes persecuted unmercifully, this unique grassland rodent that ranchers despise and shooters love to kill for fun is an extremely interesting one, an animal given to more than a few idiosyncrasies. For starters, prairie dogs have a complex vocabulary. All those squeaks, yips, and barks have meaning, biologists say, with *Cynomys ludovicianus* appearing to be as communicative as it is social.

The basis of prairie dog society is the coterie, a family group generally consisting of a dominant male, three or four breeding age females and possibly a half-dozen non-breeding juveniles. Each coterie is highly territorial, and researchers have recorded battles over territory fought by pregnant females that lasted as long as six hours. The young are born in early spring following a 33-38 day gestation period. Litters average three pups, with each individual weighing in at a scant half ounce at birth. The pups, born naked, begin to acquire fur in three weeks. Eyes open about two weeks later.

When the pups make their presence known above ground they're social and playful, while the adults remain watchful and hungry. Birth control in dog towns is family business, practiced by lactating female kin within individual coteries. Given the opportunity, sisters, half sisters, mothers, and daughters kill and consume offspring born within the family group. Biologists speculate that the reason is simple nutrition. Females nurse pups for six weeks or so, and successful mothers are those that can best feed their families. A meal of purloined pup adds protein to the diet, and possibly a few hard to get minerals. Instances of partial infanticide have been recorded, and coterie members regularly consume infants that young mothers abandon. Also, adult males seeking new territory have been known to kill pups, much like other animals ranging from house cats to grizzly bears.

So, even for the cute little prairie dogs that tourists love to ogle, survival comes down to food and food quality. The same pertains to grazers like buffalo, known to spend as much as 56 percent of their time foraging along the borders of dog towns. Bison consume mostly grass, along with a minor percentage of forbs and shrubs. Prairie dogs are quick to do bison a favor and remove the taller forbs and woody vegetation from the periphery of their towns, fearing that shrubby growth could conceal predators. The buffalo, in turn, take advantage of additional grazing that's still green, succulent and tender.

In one study, prairie dogs numbering from eight to 12 per acre reduced the grass biomass by about 40 percent compared to study plots that remained dogless. Forbs growing in the plots occupied by prairie dogs were mostly untouched by the chubby little groundskeepers. Cattle allowed to graze in both the dog town pastures and in dogless study plots put on weight at about the same rate in both; researchers observed that in the dog towns, the steers gained by eating more forbs, a class of plants generally high in protein.

Before Columbus, the dog towns would have attracted buffalo to the grass, pronghorns to the forbs, and both in great numbers. Studies combining prairie dogs, bison and/or cattle have shown that, while prairie dogs defoliate much of the grass growing in and near their colonies, plant roots compensate by distributing more nutrients to remaining stems and leaves in an effort to spur new growth. The result is more protein delivered in more easily digestible greenery for buffalo and cattle alike. In time, and under repeated close grazing, grass plant root systems weaken and forbs move in and eventually take over. That's the point when buffalo and prairie dogs once moved on to greener pastures, leaving behind excellent forage for the browsers programmed to move in when the dog towns moved on. Plants that didn't appeal to prairie dogs and bison remain a pronghorn antelope's super salad. So the antelope grew fat, and in time grass returned to dominance and the prairie dogs and buffalo moved back again. The only thing that didn't fit into this well-adjusted natural equation was pioneers with barbed wire, cattle, and a penchant for poisoning anything that seemed to be in the way...

(*Previous page*) West Cache Creek gathers strength before tumbling over a series of stair-stepping waterfalls that carve the granite chasm known as the Narrows. (*This page*) Clouds like these, building during a spring afternoon, can be as dangerous as they are ominous. The granite outcrops, prairie meadows and islands of oak trees are no strangers to the power of Oklahoma tornados.

(*Top*) A bull elk, strips of summer's protective velvet still dangling from his autumn antlers, takes a break from a boisterous morning of battling to keep his harem intact. (*Bottom*) The Medicine Bluffs bordering the refuge on nearby Fort Sill were a spiritual retreat for the Kiowa and Comanche who came here to fast, pray, seek divine guidance and medicinal healing power.

Gaillardia, or Indian Blanket, carpets refuge meadows in late spring. The common name refers to its bright colors, resembling the wool blankets still preferred by local Native Americans for ceremonial events.

This natural reflecting pool at the entrance to the refuge's Charon's Garden Wilderness shines mirror clear on a late winter afternoon.

(*Top*) A summer storm turns the horizon an eerie shade of yellow and tousles the topknot of a veteran buffalo bull. (*Bottom*) Small and secretive, Texas brown snakes are hard to spot amid the oak woods and grassy meadows dotting the refuge. In late summer females bear live young. (*Facing page*) The purple fruits of prickly pear cactus add to a granite outcrop montage overlooking Osage Lake.

(*Facing page*) Granite rocks rest amid the tools that gave them shape over eons: the freeze-thaw action resulting from ice storms and the lowly lichens that wear away at the surface while adding a touch of abstract art. (*Top*) The refuge's north entrance is guarded by Mount Sheridan, named for a famed cavalry officer. The mountain was once a dream quest site for the plains warriors he battled. (*Left*) Millions of years of erosion have resulted in rock formations that defy the imagination in the Wichitas' jumble of giant granite boulders.

(*Top*) The diamondback rattlesnake, or "coontail" of western folklore, is a common resident of the rocky Wichitas and plays an important role in the ecology of this unique terrain. (*Bottom*) An itch that needs scratching is all it takes for a buffalo bull to begin the process of hollowing out a favorite wallow. (*Facing page*) Bailey's lace cactus is small and mostly unnoticeable where it grows among granite outcrops. Then spring arrives and the electric magenta of the flowers flashes like neon against lichen-streaked stone.

(*Facing page*) Baptisia found in the Wichitas ranges in color from the rich purple-blue to creamy white to pale yellow to the nearly neon gold of Baptisia sphaerocarpa. (*Top*) The Wichitas retain a remnant herd of the famed longhorn cattle that marched north to market across the western edge of the mountain range over the Great Western Cattle Trail of cowboy folklore. (*Left*) By mid-November the season's first frosts turn switchgrass seedheads silver while whitetail bucks spar for mates throughout the cool mornings.

(*Right*) September rains lead to Indian Summer days when water once more runs in refuge streams and elk announce their ardor to misty dawns. (*Bottom*) January ice may threaten domestic livestock off the refuge, but buffalo tend to take bad weather in stride due to the insulating properties of their winter coats.

(*Top*) May thunderstorms can seem menacing, but they provide vital moisture needed to nourish prairie grasses and legumes needed by refuge grazers. (*Left*) The handsome blue flowers of this legume dot the greening prairie landscape around the time buffalo calves are born.

Standing cypress, *Ipomopsis rubra,* is an imposing member of the phlox family that can grow six feet tall. This early summer member of the Wichita Mountains flora features vivid scarlet flowers.

On the fourth day of June, wild residents of the Wichitas were celebrating a wet spring by eating their fill, unmindful of the destructive forces once unleashed upon them by a nation bent upon replicating the European landscapes their forefathers once fled. The weather was seasonably warm, the humidity high, and the sheer essence of life within the refuge almost oozing following ample and strategically delivered rainfall. A few extremely flat, thin-soiled acres dotted with buffalo wallows held a lush growth of grama grass, more so than I'd ever seen in years past, and the buffalo grazing there appeared fatter because of it.

But that's what a warm and rainy spring can do. Camera in hand, I wandered away from the prairie dog town to snap a few frames of a tall, blonde, and brown cousin to the coneflowers, a *rudebeckia* commonly known as black-eyed Susan. Background color grew in shades of grass green, purple, and pink, the latter including poppy mallows and the beautiful, pink *Sabatia campanulata*, or rose gentian.

Drooping seeds atop wild rye grass stems were turning brown, as late winter and early spring greenery prepared to broadcast seeds to the wind and go dormant for another year. The tall wild mint *monarda* reminded me of a pagoda in pale pink, the multi-tiered petals sloping like eaves on some Japanese religious sanctuary. Leadplant, a bushy forb with gray foliage and small, bright purple and yellow flowers, hosted a slew of insects, joining in the pollination effort with purple prairie clover, a flower that reminds me of a pale green thimble in a bright purple tutu. The influx of insects is the bane of summer, all those annoying biting flies and mosquitoes. However they all tend to taste the same to great-crested flycatchers "singing" from nearby oaks, their voices like metal scraping metal. A brighter background music included bobwhite quail whistling their namesake calls, the dapper black, white, and russet males hoping to attract a nesting and chick-rearing partner.

A small green hawk moth appeared to glory in a simpler life, motoring like a miniature helicopter from flower to flower, sipping from what must seem like an endless supply of nectar. June is warm, drowsy, full of life, and very good in a wet year, especially so, it seemed, for the big buffalo bull rubbing away the last of his winter coat on a boulder that's the only thing above ground level in the middle of a large prairie. Not far away, a small band of bulls look as if they've been hosed down with mud. Wallowing helps keep the biting flies at bay, and these guys should survive their afternoon naps without irritation.

At mid-month, on a cool, overcast morning following another series of thunderstorms, I drove a few miles north of the refuge to Rainy Mountain, a low knob that barely qualifies as a hill, much less a mountain, yet remains a landmark on this flat plain. It was time to pay homage to a man whose words have become the bedrock poetry of this place, the voice of a people who discovered the horse and the chase when they migrated to the Southern Plains, and a final homeplace here in the shadows of the Wichitas.

The Rainy Mountain area is where the Kiowa Indian grandparents of writer N. Scott Momaday took their 160-acre allotment when the Kiowa reservation was abolished and much of the land opened for white settlement in 1901. Momaday, born in a nearby federal Indian hospital to Kiowa artist and educator Al Momaday and writer/educator Natachee Scott, wrote of his early years spent near Rainy Mountain with his Kiowa-speaking grandparents and other relatives in *The Way to Rainy Mountain*, a book tracing the physical and cultural exodus of the Kiowa people from a homeland in the northern Rockies to the prairies bordering the Wichita Mountains.

Momaday has written of how the heritage of his Kiowa people and the landscape that shaped it coexist, pointing out that the bond is formed by "the way that we look at a given landscape and take possession of it in our blood and brain. None of us lives apart from the land entirely; such an isolation is unimaginable. If we are to realize and maintain our humanity, we must come to a moral comprehension of earth and air as it is perceived in the long turn of seasons and of years."

At least "once in our lives we ought to concentrate our minds upon the remembered earth," Momaday observed. "We ought to give ourselves up to a particular landscape in our experience, to look at it from as many angles as we can, to wonder about it, to dwell upon it. We ought to imagine that we touch it with our hands at every season, and listen to the sounds that are made upon it. We ought to imagine the creatures there and all the faintest motions of the wind. We ought to recollect the glare of noon and all the colors of the dawn and dusk." He could have added that in modern times, it would be impossible to do these things without wilderness areas and wildlife refuges.

Today you still see Momaday's love of place in the faces of Kiowa and Comanche Indian children who come to these mountains on weekends to stare at the antics of prairie dogs and listen to the roar of bison bulls preparing to do battle beneath a warm June sun. You wonder if a genetic memory is in place, a blood history that allows them to feel the ground thunder as the buffalo herds of yesteryear scatter and the hooves of horses pound the prairie turf, the hunts a ballet of blood and bravery, fear and survival. These are the progeny of Kicking Bird and Lone Wolf, Satank and Satanta. Proud people who drew nourishment and spiritual strength from this landscape, and in doing so gave these children the gift of a history still living in the earth beneath their feet, and the wild creatures that roam upon it.

When Quaker missionary Thomas C. Battey arrived in 1871 to convert the Kiowa to Christianity, he wrote in his book *The Life and*

Adventures of a Quaker Among the Indians, that "nothing in the way of pure land scenery could be more picturesque than this elevated prairie, surrounded by huge rocks, pile upon pile, with here and there a stunted cedar, struggling for life and a scanty foothold in the fissures by which they are rifted. These, rising as they do several hundred feet above us, in every conceivable form of serrated crags, present an outline against the clear vault of heaven equally striking with the most fanciful sketch the pencil ever traced."

Riding south into the Wichitas, Battey noted, "our route today was . . . over a plain covered with mesquite timber and bounded by isolated mountains. . . We continued on nearly south until about noon when, being in the midst of many thousands of buffalo, which were occupied, some in leisurely grazing, some in wallowing and rolling in the dust, some in fighting but most in wild, impetuous flight."

When he wrote these words Battey was in the midst of what had once been the great southern buffalo herd. Within a decade, almost all these animals would be dead, killed for their hides by market hunters. Bison played such a vital role in the Kiowa lifestyle that the animals were centerpiece to an annual spiritual revival held in June. Sometimes referred to as a Sun Dance, Battey called this Kiowa celebration of renewal the Great Medicine Dance, and was fortunate to attend the 1872 gathering held on a stream not far from the Wichitas.

It seems that this weeklong observation of religious reunification Battey witnessed was about as lavish, in its own way, as a coronation of a pope. There was prayer, dance, theater, and even comedy, all performed according to a script passed down by memory. The 1872 dance stretched from June 16 to June 21, so in part it was an observation of the Summer Solstice as well as an old-fashioned camp meeting done Kiowa style. Battey said all the Kiowa bands were there, along with some 500 Comanche, nearly all of the Kiowa-Apache, and some visiting Cheyenne and Arapaho.

"I was round among them most of the time by day," Battey pointed out in chapter 10 of his memoir. "I saw not a single instance of disagreement. On the contrary, everything moved on harmoniously and quietly, and the tribes dispersed with apparently friendly feelings."

The missionary also mentioned that, when the leafy branches forming the shady roof of the dance arbor began to wilt, "To-haint, the great medicine chief, made medicine for clouds and rain. The rain came, with a tempest of wind and the most vivid lightning. Peal after peal of thunder shook the air. The ground literally flooded."

Battey added that two Cheyenne women were killed by the lightning, and that To-haint apologized. He said he was "a young man, and had no idea of making such strong medicine."

Good medicine for modern times, as well as modern hearts and minds, are the mid-June trails leading back into Charon's Garden, the refuge wilderness area. As the Summer Solstice approaches they're etched in windswept gold, and it's easy to understand why June has long been a time of homecoming and spiritual renewal. Calliopsis, a flower similar to the bright yellow coreopsis that blanketed the refuge just weeks before, is the same vivid yellow except for just a touch of deep red in the center. Almost as widespread as the coreopsis had been, the flowers reach skyward under a strengthening June sun and glow and glisten like the shallow lakes in the distance. Patches of orange-yellow prairie coneflowers complete the Summer Solstice color scheme. All that's lacking is the laughter of women, the howling of camp dogs, swarms of naked children playing by the creek, and tipis.

Today the refuge prairie dogs are so fat they look like footballs with heads attached. They seem to waddle rather than walk, a sign that the spring economy has been good and that the colony has made a smart investment in storing fat for the rigors of the winter to come. The pups, on the other hand, are like urchins on a playground, too active to store up much of anything other than lessons in life. They wrestle with each other, then break for quality family time, grooming with the adults and exchanging the customary "kiss," which in reality is more a test of prairie dog halitosis that identifies who's who.

Clumps of bluestem grasses that haven't been mowed and maintained by prairie dogs and buffalo are knee-high now, and taking on a bluish namesake tint to better regulate the strengthening rays of the sun. Wood nymph butterflies, cruising low on fawn brown wings bearing large, yellow-ringed eyespots, fly over the grasses that have given them life: bluestem serves as host plants for the larva. Milkweed seed capsules, some the size of small bananas, have turned brown, split open and allowed seeds attached to soft, silvery white, threadlike filaments to escape skyward. The downy attachments let the seeds soar like tiny baskets slung under shiny balloons, riding the wind without restraint. If the seeds fall to the ground in a spot receptive to a new milkweed plant, so be it. Otherwise, few other seeds are entitled to experience such a ride.

A cool north wind blowing on the morning of June 26 simply means that the heat will be held back for a few, blissful hours. Otherwise the high 80s or low 90s are now customary each day, and the shrill buzz of cicadas calling from the shade of oak groves announces the upcoming season. Cicada song is the summer anthem here, a vibrating roar that goes up with the mercury. A stream in the wilderness backcountry still trickles, but the flood of sunlight has resulted in pools filled with long strands of algae. Walking into the wilderness, I flush five does, coats sleek and smooth now, pale brown rather than gray. An obviously worried turkey hen clucks nervously and ducks through low brush growing beneath the streamside elms. Poults are hidden somewhere nearby.

A waterfall that was thundering over a ledge just weeks ago now flows like a faucet left carelessly dripping. The pool that catches this trickle also catches the small leopard frogs that leap away at my approach. Judging from their numbers, all that late March and early April cacophonous chatter must have been truly irrepressible love song.

The heat builds quickly on the last day of June, and the sun illuminates a world of rich, deep shading. Orange rock glistens above yellow flowers, the boulders set against a blue that's almost black and framed in a shade of green that screams summer. A mixed herd of several dozen buffalo march down for a drink, their grunts and mumbles sounding like farmers meeting in a small town café for their morning coffee. Both bulls and cows walk through a patch of ironweed, a dark purple flower atop a stalk that reaches to the shoulders of most of the calves. Ironweed is a summer flower, a plant that loves July heat, long afternoons, and a variety of insect pollinators. A huge bull in the prime of life, as sleek from summer shedding as a newly sheared Marine recruit, stops to roll on the dirt mounds of a dog town, then climbs to his feet and scratches with a hind hoof like a dog with an itch. Another bull, older and scruffier, has something on his mind other than dusty hygiene. When a cow urinates he immediately checks the smell, raising his massive head and curling back a lip like a stallion testing a mare's receptivity. This cow's hormones aren't quite up to a passing score, but soon. And that's when dust will rise over the sounds of battle.

SUMMER WARRIOR. Seasonally scarred and battle tested, a buffalo bull in his prime fights to assert his dominance.

July

It's a hot July day in the Wichitas, and a buffalo bull, sleek, fat, and the color of a chocolate brownie, has retired to the shade of a solitary oak for a siesta. The afternoon high temperature will reach the mid-90s, and the time for grazing and strolling to water was much earlier, with the sunrise. Midday summertime on the Southern Plains is made for drowsing and maybe watching the wind encourage wildflowers to dance. Sons and daughters of white settlers still work through the heat of the day here, but the indigenous people followed the example of the wild creatures around them and were active when the shadows were long. July is a time to appreciate the sun and also respect it. Common sense says life should be placed on hold at its zenith; activity resumes when the sun's angles are less overpowering, or put off entirely until the intense red orb drops below the edge of the Earth.

A visitor wouldn't need a calendar to ascertain that July has a grip on this land of orange rock and sweeping, blue-tinted grasses. This morning the view from a mountaintop was almost as hazy as you'd find in West Virginia, indicating that a steady south breeze has delivered ample Gulf moisture. The humidity makes the refuge feel even hotter. Sweat doesn't dry, and clothes grow saturated. The humidity also indicates that these low mountains don't belong ecologically with those of the high desert grasslands of Arizona and New Mexico. There the evaporation rate is much higher, the nights cooler, the plants and animals more arid-adapted. These prairies are, when the rain gods manage to keep up with the averages, a little too wet to fit in with a cultural motif featuring adobe bricks and red chilies. As proof, a combination of humidity and afternoon heating has a thunderhead billowing up on the northern horizon. The huge pillar of a cloud, resembling white and gray cotton balls stacked one atop another, reverberates thunder like a giant stomach growling. Streaks of lightning split the dark core, and soon it's evident that the grasslands need to hold their cups out and upward—it's going to rain.

I don't know if the buffalo and elk understand that the rain means nourishment in the form of new, tender growth, but the four bull elk resting on the prairie seem happy enough with the approaching weather. Rain is the elixir of grazing animals, a promise in liquid form that their bellies will stay full, that fat will cling to their bones and provide energy reserves for winter. Suburban Americans may see grass as something that must be mowed and kept uniform, a monospecies swath where broad-leaved plants are the enemy. Theirs is a mini-environment where artificial fertilization and watering are necessary and every bug, weed, and burrowing animal is attacked with poisons that tend to hang around long after their application. Here in the refuge, disarray is the bliss of hundreds of species evolving, cooperating, competing and, in the end, prospering due to the toughness that comes from evolutionary struggle and eventual species success.

Grass in the Wichitas is more of an extended family, a family with a few warts in the form of invasive species, yet at the core a family that's adjusted to the demands of weather, insects, microscopic plants and animals, small mammals and large ones, the threat of frost, the fury of fire. It's a wild family at heart and a tough one, given half a chance and a little understanding.

Grasslands live and die according to rules adapted and perfected over thousands of years, essentially since the end of the last Ice Age. According to ecologist J. E. Weaver, writing in his book *Prairie Plants and Their Environment*, "After thousands of years, the species have adjusted to their environment. The plants, with few exceptions, are remarkably free from disease, regardless of the weather, and are little injured by high winds or extreme heat. . . Those that were unfit have disappeared and those that remain have reacted to the factors of the environment so thoroughly that as species, they successfully meet the most severe conditions."

As a result, the prairies and plains are blessed with hundreds of species of grasses and forbs that interact to provide healthy living space for birds, reptiles, mammals, and amphibians, no matter their size. The proof is as plain as the field of view stretching out before me on a bright Wichita Mountains morning: comparing the refuge and its living components to one of the many wheat fields beyond the fence is the difference between Noah's Ark and an empty rowboat abandoned on a beach.

Healthy grasslands make for healthy bison, and the heat of summer here on the refuge means that bulls are of a mind to mate with healthy cows and create a healthy future in the form of reddish orange calves, many at the moment demanding nourishment with a butt of their determined baby heads directed at the udders of their taciturn mothers. The sleek bull napping in the shade of the oak is a totally different creature when the scent of a lady friend tells him it's time to procreate. At that moment he's a ton of total determination on the hoof, willing to fight and kill to pass his genes on to the next generation.

A battle between two tons of angry bull buffalo is a spectacle reminiscent of when dinosaurs walked the earth. It can be pure savagery, yet is mostly predicated on lots of pawing, bellowing, and bluffing; biology allows the young, the weak, the elderly, and the uncertain an opportunity to bow out before the actual clash of head and horns. Fighting is serious business, draining energy reserves, risking injury and even death. Therefore those that engage in this ritual warfare have evolved an escape clause that insures a certain amount of longevity, essentially time to learn on the job.

Dale F. Lott, bison researcher and author of *American Bison: A Natural History,* writes in part 1, chapter 1 that when bulls clash "heads come together with a terrific shock. It ripples through their bodies in a visible wave." He adds "I once saw a bull somersaulted backward by such a charge: 2,000 pounds of bull flipped upside down like a lawn chair in a gust of wind."

Mature bulls have a thick mat of hair over the crown and forehead to absorb some of the impact, and, as Lott points out, most challenges seem to be elaborate tests of the opponent's determination, ending without a fight. Many fights are little more than pushing and shoving without the delivery of lethal uppercuts. Subtle signs of submission generally are respected, and the match ends quickly. For younger bulls, mating is a learning process that may not be fulfilled immediately. The ability to bow out of a fight without penalty allows younger animals the opportunity to both attend class and live through it. Older bulls, on the other hand, grasp that time isn't on their side and are prone to fight to the finish as they seek one more opportunity to sire offspring before searching for that little green pasture in which to lie down.

A summer day at the refuge may reveal several bulls sparring simply because their hormones tell them to. Oftentimes cows aren't even in the picture—it's just that the breeding season inspires a powerful urge to dominate. Actual breeding happens when cows in estrus release hormones that signal it's time. Bulls read the readiness of cows with the aid of their vomernasal organ, accessed through the roof of the mouth. Testing includes sampling a cow's urine, elevating the head, curling the upper lip and ample tongue fluttering. If the bull begins to "tend" the cow, essentially staying with, protecting and watching her every move, more than likely actual coupling is soon to follow.

Cows coming into estrus tend to be restless, a trait that bulls watch for and congregate around. In time a dominant bull emerges, the cow is ready, and the future of the buffalo nation is renewed in four or five seconds. The process is more Battle of the Titans than Shakespeare, but ample evidence that the system is working are all these calves, now in the process of changing from rust-red youngsters that resemble the calves of domestic cattle into chocolate brown facsimiles of their older herd mates.

Cow bison mostly go unnoticed while bulls steal the stage with their displays of brute strength. However, cows have their own hierarchy, and dominant cows tend to get more of the best grazing and therefore deliver healthier calves come springtime. Cows generally start to dominate others at a certain level of maturity and tend to stay dominant until about eight years of age, when physical decline begins to reverse the process. As bison biologists explain, subordinate cows have to search harder for food and end up with less. Each cow is attempting to eat enough to trigger ovulation and then provide for a developing fetus through winter's lean months. When forage is scarce, as in drought years, dominant cows have a distinct nutritional advantage.

Grazers live or die according to the rules of a "fat economy" that demands continuous consumption of available forage in spring and summer, so that fat can be stored to provide energy when the plant world goes dormant with waning sunlight. It helps that bison can slow their metabolism rate in the winter, something that can't be said for imported cattle, which require supplemental feeding. Bison, on the other hand, are much better equipped for survival, from their sunlight-absorbing dark hair to their ability to slow down the body furnace when calories aren't available.

A July sun on the Southern Plains can stifle energy and ambition among both four-legged and two-legged, especially those who fail to heed its radiant power. A single afternoon spent in the open on a 100-degree day can be torture for those unaccustomed to the searing dominance of our life-giving star's radiation. Buffalo, evolved to a life in the open, simply pick a spot where the breeze blows best and take it easy. Hikers wear a hat. Native grasses readjust the photosynthetic process, curl or unfurl leaves or change angles to control the amount of sunlight flooding over their foliage. At times the force of the sun can seem extreme, but the natives know how to cope with it. After all, a buffalo is nothing more than the sunlight that grew the grass that fed the grazer that's busily ruminating on a hillside where a breeze keeps the flies at bay. Sunlight, it seems, even the bright sunlight of a Southern Plains July, is a basic fact of grassland life.

The bison taking it easy on the sunny slope is turning grass to meat by converting cellulose to carbohydrates with the aid of multiple stomachs and the bacteria that live within them. Grass plants are constantly on the defensive—they don't want to be eaten, and would rather grow abundantly, develop ample leafy appendages to intercept sunlight and covert it to sugars, and eventually raise a flower stalk into the wind and scatter seed. At the same time roots and rhizomes—the bulk of a prairie grass plant—are storing the food that will be needed to break dormancy in the spring and compete with all the other grasses and forbs vying for the same sunlight, moisture, and minerals.

Therefore the grasses evolve strategies to render themselves less digestible. Buffalo, on the other hand, rely upon symbiotic bacteria to evolve an even better system of breaking down cellulose faster than the plants can make the task more difficult. Bison have the upper hand in this ongoing contest in that bacteria, capable of producing several generations a day, evolve faster than grasses can come up with new defensive strategies.

The actual work done deep in the folds of a buffalo's gut essentially amounts to fermentation, the same process that takes a sack of grain and turns it into beer. Bacteria break down grasses into carbohydrates and fatty acids. This takes place in the first and largest of the multi-chambered stomach, the rumen. After the initial treatment, bison turn to their own enzymes to further digest the results. A certain percentage of the bacteria also end up as buffalo fodder in the process, enlarging the scope and scale of available nutrients.

This formula of sun, grass, bacteria, and evolution has produced an animal that's capable of outrunning a racehorse for several hundred yards and a standing high jump approaching six feet—feats that can't be equaled by Old Bessie the barnyard bovine.

However, this highly successful species wasn't without natural population control parameters. Cyclic drought on the plains could reduce forage productivity by as much as 90 percent in certain regions. Some biologists believe that bands of buffalo wolves following the herds may have taken as much as a third of the annual calf crop, and severe winters have been known to reduce Yellowstone National Park bison numbers by 30 percent.

The vast bison herds of yesteryear competed with hordes of plant-devouring grasshoppers, plus tiny nematodes in the dirt beneath their feet that consumed more of the prairie plants than all herbivores and grass-eating insects put together. Buffalo did their part to nourish what they ate by providing free urine and feces, and lots of both—prime fertilizer made easily available to the grasses by adding water in the form of rainfall.

Bison are patch grazers, returning again and again to spots where they've kept the grass short and green, or in buffalo vocabulary, tender and nutritious. In doing so they create diversity, something generally missing from cattle pasture. When researchers at the Tallgrass Prairie Preserve in northern Oklahoma began experimental burning to determine the reactions of more than 2,000 bison there, the result was the familiar patchwork quilt of "golf green " patterns amid old, bleached dormant grasses. And, when these patches of new green growth were created with the aid of prescribed fire, the buffalo came to them like insects seeking spring flowers.

None of the biologists were able to figure out how the animals knew that tender grass was available, but they did—and oftentimes traveled miles to sample the savory fare. The biologists, following bison with GPS tracking devices, discovered that the grazers set out across country in a hurry when freshly burned areas became available. One of the researchers actually said that the buffalo moved to the burns like "bees to honey," but was at a loss to explain the animals' maneuvers. Some speculated that the herds went to the smell of smoke. Others thought they might key in on the movement of birds and insects.

The researchers also found that the patchwork patterns created by fire over the years resulted in a variety of vegetative characteristics. New burns contained different species than old burns, and each attracted its own unique variety of birds and insects. These experiments suggest that historically, the prairies and plains of yesteryear were much more species-rich than today's native grassland remnants. The original grazers sculpted a mosaic that changed with the years and seasons, providing variety as complex as the plains' weather moods and rainfall. Today's painfully species-deficient grasslands pale before what surely must have been, that vast natural quilt of abundant, specialized life ranging from bacteria to buffalo.

Biologists delving into bison mysteries also found that buffalo hair was the most prominent material used in the nests of grassland birds. Nearly 50 percent of the nests they checked at the prairie preserve contained wool from the humpbacked grazers. Also, these frequent wallowers were found to be the "Johnny Appleseeds" of grasslands. Bison hair samples contained 2,768 seeds from some 76 plant species. Grass seeds comprised about half of those found in both dung and hair samples, indicating that these salad eaters were, inadvertently, playing an important role in growing their own.

True native grassland or prairie, or what little is left of it, is a dynamically intertwined system, coexisting and competing much like the creatures inhabiting the open air, but without an ambulatory option. Plants put down roots. Thus the adjustments they make to environmental factors tend to be chemical rather than mobility-oriented. In the stand-your-ground world of a prairie plant, change is both necessary and a long time coming.

A zoology professor friend of mine once quizzed his class by asking which is the more complex ecosystem, woodland or prairie. The students eagerly answered woodland, and the professor then devoted the session to proving them wrong.

He was aided by the fact that America's grasslands have a history of being under appreciated, over utilized and patently misunderstood. Even many ranchers, whose livelihoods depend upon how grasses react to grazing pressure and drought, look upon all grasses as the same and only care that cattle can and will eat what's there until it is gone.

Sadly, that's why some ranches go bankrupt. Not just because of drought, a routine fact of life on the plains that generally gets the blame for failing ranchland economics. Prairie plants are adapted to withstand drought and eventually recover. What they can't bounce back from is years of consumptive abuse that weakens and destroys the underlying root systems, allowing the invasion of noxious grasses and forbs or woody, thorny vegetation rarely palatable to beef cattle.

Healthy grassland offers nourishment to livestock by providing as many as 200 native plant species per square mile. These species coexist by sharing the soil at various levels, sunlight at varying heights and sun, and moisture and essential nutrients at varying seasons. And, even though the competition is fierce, plant variety helps boost overall survival: legumes add nitrogen to the soil that benefits the entire plant community. Taller plants protect shorter ones from excessive sunlight, while plants that form a low, ground-hugging mat act as mulch that preserves soil moisture.

In his book *Prairie Plants and their Environment: A Fifty Year Study in the Midwest*, grassland ecologist J. E. Weaver explained it thusly: "The beauty and quiet calm of the grassland should not obscure the fact that the prairie is both a field of battle that is centuries old and a field in which the conflicting species, never wholly victorious nor entirely vanquished, each year renew their struggle." Each native species arms itself for this ageless combat by deploying a deep, efficient root system, including root bulbs and rhizomes that store energy to boost rapid growth at the start of the growing season. Prairie plants also depend upon vegetative reproduction featuring rhizome tillers and root sprouts that spread out beneath the surface and serve as an anchor for new plants that push upward from underground buds.

Climax grassland, Weaver said, when grazed lightly or moderately, can generally retain its natural condition over extremely long periods. "It is only when grazing animals are circumscribed in their range by fences, and when too large a population is thus confined, that grazing and trampling becomes so excessive that the normal cover cannot be maintained."

The former professor at the University of Nebraska cautioned that if plants favored by grazers are cropped too early, too often, or too closely they disappear entirely. At this point invading plants do what they do best, attacking the weakening native system and gaining a foothold. Unfortunately, the invading species are rarely as palatable or productive as the plants they've replaced.

Grassland in the Wichitas is mostly midgrass prairie, intermediate between the tallgrass and shortgrass types lying east and west and separated by as much as 20 inches of annual rainfall. Bluestem grasses are common to this grassland comprised of both eastern and western species, and can represent as much as 75 percent of the total plant cover. Bluestems are a widespread and extremely successful species, well adapted to drought and grazing pressure and capable of explosive growth under favorable conditions.

Of the two, big bluestem is most often found where the soil is deeper and moisture more readily available. In a rainy year coupled with little or no grazing, solid stands of big bluestem can grow seven to nine feet tall. From mid- to late-summer the flower stems show pale pastels, the joints or internodes sometimes turning a soft pink, while others are a pale blue-green. By late autumn the stems may turn a rich wine red, a dazzling sight when mingling with the bright golden seed plumes of Indian grass.

Both bluestems erupt with new growth when the season turns wet and warm. A big bluestem seedling may begin to spread underground roots in seven to eight weeks, and soon afterward may send up shoots from subterranean buds. Little bluestem quickly obtains six to eight inches in height if spring weather remains favorable and soon begins to tiller profusely, forming the distinct bunchy growth the species prefers.

Little bluestem survives better on thinner, droughty soils, and may provide as much as 60 to 90 percent of the grass cover on uplands. Both grasses survive on the strength of extensive root systems. Big bluestem roots probe deeply, the coarse, fibrous underground growth reaching six to eight feet deep and mining water beyond the reach of many other grasses. Little bluestem's roots are finer and more spreading, designed to both reach deeply for water at five feet or so, and also extend an ambitious network to capture rainfall from sudden, short summer thunderstorms that may soak in just a few inches deep.

Bluestem rhizomes can live many years, and the sons and daughters of ranchers who cut hay from a bluestem meadow may continue to harvest growth from the same plants for decades. The gleanings of the hay baler, cut in early July when the plant is nutritionally prime, is an excellent winter food source for cattle throughout the range of the bluestem prairie. And, while the hay bales are tangible representatives of the prairie's bounty, they represent but a fraction of the total grass system. A strip of prairie sod four inches deep, eight inches wide and 100 inches long contains a tangled network of roots, buds, and rhizomes that would extend more than 20 miles if unraveled. Plants like the bluestems truly are masters of their universe, evolved to survive attacks from both above and below, manage drought and live to a ripe old age in the process.

It's been said that the best way to learn about the prairie is on your hands and knees. But on this sun-soaked July day, some of the most interesting plants are flowering head high or higher. Compass plant, *Silphium laciniatum*, sun-loving and among the more regal of the aster family, is in bloom on a patch of prairie near a grove of oaks where several bison seek shelter from the afternoon heat. It's a handsome, stately plant, with stems that may grow as tall as big bluestem and generally stand stout and straight, rough and hairy, and filled with resinous sap. The flower is such a bright yellow that it seems to be sliced from a shaft of summer sunlight. The leaves, large and deeply lobed, twist to follow the sun during its sweltering arch, thus the common name.

Compass plant survives this blazing, desiccating season with the help of a taproot that may reach as deeply as those of the tallgrasses. Like the majority of midsummer prairie forbs, compass plant comes in one color—bright butter yellow. And, if this were strictly cattle pasture, odds are these tall stems would be grazed much shorter, or even nonexistent. While cattle will dine on forbs and grow fat on them, buffalo prefer grass. Therefore the shimmering image of bison and tall yellow flowers sharing space has an aura of history about it. At the moment a massive bull, up and grazing following his siesta, has his oft-battered head at ground level, sorting green grass leaves from among coarser selections, all within inches of a grove of compass plant that he's chosen to ignore. In this case the term grove seems apt, considering that these lovely flowers are perched atop stout stalks rising well above the bull's massive hump, and seem more like slim shrubs than wildflowers.

The opposite of the compass plant's towering solidarity is the pale lavender of low-growing ruellia flowering between my feet, an exception to the rule of thumb that midsummer flowers on the Southern Plains are mostly yellow. Ruellia, oftentimes called wild petunia, escapes some of the overpowering blast of sunlight by flowering amid the little bluestem bunches, or tussocks, allowing its prairie compatriots to provide vital shade.

The sun is intense by seven in the morning, and bison are ambling to prairie dog towns to snip away at their breakfast. Most have finished grazing by 10 in the morning, about the time that the heat becomes uncomfortable. Buffalo have little problem with stretching out in full sunlight and allowing a south breeze to both cool them somewhat and also keep a few of the biting flies at bay. Domestic cattle, on the other hand, will stack up in the shade of a single tree if one's available, or stand brisket deep in their water source for hours at a time, defecating, urinating, trampling banks to bare dirt and generally destroying any aquatic area they have access to.

On the afternoon of July 27 the buffalo get a short reprieve from the heat. The mountains are surrounded with clouds, a low, dark gray ceiling that seems destined to clabber into at least a temperature-easing shower. But the weather moods remain fickle and rain falls all around the refuge, yet nary a drop on it. The bison take the near miss in stride, but panting crows seem extra fussy.

But that's the nature of storms produced by afternoon heating. They rise unpredictably, dump moisture haphazardly, and dissipate quickly. In the days before roads and fences, the buffalos' restless meanders would have allowed them to follow the rain and reap the benefits of the spotty downpours. Today's fenced herds have to depend upon luck rather than mobility.

Fortunately luck is in store some 72 hours later. A cool front pushing down from the north collides with July heat and humidity, spawning showers, rain-cooled air, and afternoon temperatures that barely edge into the 80s. Such readings seem divine, especially under the shade of big, lumpy, gray-and-white clouds and a cooling breeze compliments of Canada.

Animals that have mostly slumbered through the heat are more active, as are those of us who, cameras in hand, have driven here to watch them. The afternoon light, more concentrated and less hazy, is perfect for photography and the mountains oblige by offering up picture-postcard scenes, including a small, manmade lake covered with the big oval leaves and pale yellow flowers of lotus. Rounded white flowers nearly the size of golf balls draw black and yellow tiger swallowtail butterflies to lakeside buttonbush, and two wood ducks paddle across the water, followed by their butter-yellow and brown brood. The drake retains his gaudy plumage: lots of reds, greens, and grays. The drab brown hen doesn't do much to tempt the palette of visiting artists, but then she's already accomplished her assigned task of rearing the next generation.

The sudden disappearance of the wood ducks turns my attention to a family entertaining themselves lakeside with a handful of rocks, which the adolescent boys are cheerfully lobbing at a snake at the insistence of their father. When the snake disappears the boys start looking for something else to harass, while the father busies himself searching for an object lesson in wild nature.

In a minute the man returns with a turkey vulture feather, a relic picked up where it was shed beneath a roost tree. He calls the boys into a circle around him and patiently explains about the Native American symbolism of "eagle feathers," while I do my best to abstain from laughing. Sadly, this gentleman's inability to grasp natural history is about average for the weekend visitors who arrive at the refuge hoping to experience at least a brief outdoor revival. They return home a bit more reconnected to the world around them and also rejuvenated by fresh air and exercise. Then it's back to school, office, the mall, and other aspects of suburbia that eventually erase all the good done by walking with buffalo.

Near where the snake fled for safety's sake, stout, multi-branched stalks of water hemlock bloom beside the stream, white flowers gathered in a flattened umbel several inches across. My sympathies for the demise of the Greek philosopher Socrates don't extend to sampling this poisonous plant that clings to muddy stream margins. The next four weeks, including the last two of July and the first two of August, are traditionally the hottest weeks of the year here, and temperatures that drive warm-blooded creatures into the night couldn't be better for certain flowers, some poisonous, most not, and the pollinators they summon from throughout the sun-loving insect world.

As a result, small yellow sulfur butterflies ride the wind, sweeping over pale blue carpets of grama grass with brown seeds atop flower stalks less than a foot tall. The seed cluster is curved like an eyebrow, while those climbing up the taller stalks of sideoats grama are much straighter. Both the curled and straight versions of this summer's growing season wave together in the wind, little flags celebrating the fact that here among the grasses a few managed to escape both longhorn and buffalo and make seed.

In a stream bottom in the wilderness area, a stand of big bluestem rises over my head, the flower stalks at least seven feet tall. The "turkey track" inflorescence, the colloquial name for the plant, bears tiny yellow bell-shaped flowers, in time to be both pollinated and distributed by the wind. Nearby at the water's edge an extremely coarse clump of switchgrass grows thick, tall, and very blue. The seeds on this native, atop the stalk in a large, expansive spray, are in the process of maturing under an oven of sun.

It's the last day of July and August will follow with more of the same—insufferable heat, high humidity, and a world that drones of insects. Reptiles, mammals, and birds continue to either suffer patiently or become nocturnal. However the first golden flash of flowering goldenrod, glinting in the shade of an oak savannah, hints of change. More likely than not the weather will begin to moderate in about three weeks, as active atmospheric patterns return, rainfall increases, and autumn attempts a few cautious advances. Even now, in the middle of the oppressive "dog days," a glance at the calendar reveals that the autumn equinox is approaching. Those of us familiar with this place understand that soon, elk will trumpet their war cry as the rut begins. Buffalo will leave the field of battle to them without remorse; soon it will be time to grow thick, dark coats and convert the last of the good grass to winter sustenance.

CHARON'S GARDEN. Erosion sculpted the fantastically shaped rock formations found throughout the refuge's Charon's Garden Wilderness.

August

The view from atop the refuge's Mount Scott takes in a large slice of the Southern Plains, with most that meets the eye rolled out as flat as the proverbial pancake. The exception is this jagged backbone of granite rising over 2,000 feet in elevation in places, a stark contrast to the lowland prairie below, much of it composed of rubble washed down from the mountains over millions of years.

West of the refuge the Wichitas continue to pop up and out of wheat fields and cattle pasture in a dimpled march toward the setting sun. The outcrops come to an abrupt end at Quartz Mountain State Park north of the city of Altus. Beyond that, the eye strains to encompass seemingly endless miles of gouged and eroded prairie, some of it brown and level, some sliced up and red as a rooster's comb, some with exposed layers of white gypsum rock. More than anything else as this August morning ebbs, the wind-whipped and heat-drenched grassland seems parched and in need of a drink. The effect intensifies under a furnace blast of sunlight that, at midday, robs the landscape of shadows and color.

North and east of the refuge are rounded hills with exposed layers of gray limestone rock, silent testimony to a marine origin millions of years ago. Beyond the stony Slick Hills are fingers of dwarf forest, the westernmost extension of the Crosstimbers, the last true woodland of notable size until the foothills of the Rockies, other than strips of gallery forest growing along the lonely rivers crisscrossing the plains.

The Wichitas' granite boulders appear to have been scattered like a pocketful of marbles on top of this sere landscape. The scene speaks of antiquity, a look that goes well with the quiet that's commonplace here except for sporadic artillery blasts from nearby Fort Sill. Take away a noisy Army and the refuge would be unnervingly quiet in an age of auditory madness, recalling the vast silences of the old Llanos del Cibolos, Plains of the Buffalo, known by pre-reservation Kiowa and Comanche.

However, the sounds from the artillery base are little more than Fourth of July firecrackers compared to the geologic turbulence that made this place. The geologic unrest that resulted in the landscape we see today originated around a half billion years ago, in a major Earth-building period known as the Cambrian. Some portions of the Earth's crust were elevated, others sank. Over time a portion of what is now the Southern Plains sank enough to be filled with water by adjoining oceans. Thick, sandy sediments and limey secretions were deposited where the Wichitas now rise above an otherwise level horizon.

Following a period of inactivity the region began to rumble with subterranean volcanic fury. Magma forced its way into the sediments deposited by the oceans, heating the quartz sand to form dense layers of quartzite rock within the sandstone, along with layers of the dark gray volcanic rock called gabbro.

Next the land began to rise, exposing the sediment beds to erosion and the dark veins of gabbro to the light of day. This was followed by more volcanic activity. Around 500 million years ago molten igneous rock flowed to the surface through volcanic vents.

When the molten rock cooled, it became the red granite exposed on modern Mount Scott. A coarser granitic magma also reached the surface, forming the paler rock found in Charon's Garden. Some of the molten flow reaching the surface congealed into rock resembling granite, but much more tightly grained. This rock, known as rhyolite, is also red and reveals a matrix of very fine crystals.

The literal ups and downs of the Wichitas continued over geologic time. The entire area sank again, filled with water once again and, when the ocean evaporated, left behind the limey deposits found in the Slick Hills. Then, about 300 million years ago, during what geologists refer to as the Pennsylvanian Period, the region experienced an uplift accompanied by massive folding and faulting. Great blocks of granite were shoved skyward by this activity, creating the modern Wichita Mountains. Geologists believe that the uplift resulted in a range originally much higher than the outcrops we see today. The contemporary Wichitas have been sculpted and pruned by millions of years of erosion, weathering that stripped away sediments that eventually washed into the lowlands around the base of the mountains, reducing the visible, rocky relief.

Now we're left with low yet scenic mountains, made even more dramatic by the way they seem to pop up through the gravel and cobble overlay. Wind and water have done a dramatic job of shaping this seemingly impregnable mass of stone, dazzling the mind's eye with huge boulders stacked atop one another like a child's building blocks and rivers of rock sliding down the sides of mountains. The weathering is so complete in places that it's difficult to grasp the geological explanation that the more erosion-prone materials were stripped away by wind and weather, revealing these phantasmagoric formations underneath. At such times it seems simpler to just shrug and go with the local Indian theory—a legend built around a rock-slinging deity tossing 100-ton boulders around like dice.

Some geologists estimate that, in their geological youth, the Wichitas may have towered up to 5,000 feet. Today the highest elevations top 2,400 feet, suggesting that about half the original may have been worn away. During the process the surrounding lowlands gained altitude as eroded material was deposited at the bottom, resulting in today's relief measurements of around 400 to 1,100 feet.

Still, it's spectacular relief, made even more dramatic by the abruptness in which massive amounts of stone erupt out of the earth like mushrooms in May. All in all, the scenery inspires visions of cataclysmic birth at a time beyond imagining. Such thoughts spring from factual roots; the refuge contains some of the oldest exposed rock in the region.

The antiquity of these mountains contrasts the youth of the Meers Fault, a "profound structural dislocation" separating the Wichita uplift from the Anadarko Basin to the north. The fault is visible from around Saddle Mountain just north of the refuge to a point along Cache Creek, some fifteen miles distant. Until recently scientists believed that the last activity along the fault line occurred hundreds of millions of years ago. Then a geologist took a closer look and realized that the Meers may be among the youngest faults east of the Rocky Mountains, with movement as recently as 500 to 2,000 years ago. Closer examination also caused geologists to concur that the fault could produce a magnitude seven earthquake in the future.

Those who study the Meers say the fault would be more at home in California, where young faults abound. Instead, they point out, it forms the only surface rupture found east of the Rockies. Fortunately, the Meers Fault remains a seismically quiet one, with a very small quake in 1981 the only recently recorded activity.

So, from the top of Mount Scott, a sweep of the eye scans truly ancient mountains, a geologically recent rip in the earth's crust, and the possible site of a future earthquake that would shake a lot of rock and wake up more than a few buffalo. From the time of their first contact with white men, resident Indians always said that this was a special place. Today's science confirms their point of view. Basically it remains a place where ancient mountain shadows fall on rifts in the land with the potential to shape the future; in so many ways the yin/yang of the Wichitas is both fascinating and pronounced, no matter if you're a university researcher or a Comanche medicine man.

And, while university scientists explain the region's cataclysmic past in the language of algebra and physics, native people contend that the transformational energy emanating from this mysterious pile of rock is simply "medicine," or the power of the divine.

According to William C. Meadows in his book *Kiowa Ethnogeography*, the Wichita Mountains contained places that were particularly holy, sites sought out by medicine men and healers seeking power and knowledge. The Kiowa Atah told anthropologist Alice Marriott that "anyone who seeks visions goes out alone and a spirit comes and speaks to him and tells him just how to do and that's where they get their medicine." Meadows recalls that Marriott's writings listed several locations where Kiowas frequently sought visions: the north slope of Mount Scott (where legendary chief Lone Wolf was buried in 1879); the dip between the peaks of Saddle Mountain a few miles north of the refuge; at mineral springs south of Carnegie; a large artesian spring near today's community of Hobart and on Mount Sheridan. Maybe the most spiritual place of all was Medicine Bluff southeast of the refuge, now part of the Army base Fort Sill.

The voice of the divine revealed itself to vision seekers in various ways. According to a local Indian family, an ancestor "went to get power on the side of Mt. Sheridan. . . on the fourth night a big mountain boomer (collared lizard) came. . . (and) blew its breath and he felt words come into his heart."

Meadows quotes Harlan Hall, a Kiowa, concerning religious connections to the region. "At times I am afforded the opportunity of returning to Kiowa country, the land of my rearing. I always try to take my family out to see the buffalo herd on the Wichita Mountains Wildlife Refuge. I love to look at the herd bull's eyes looking (back) at me. My grandfather told me that if you do that, it means he (the buffalo) wants to talk Kiowa with you. Kiowas and buffaloes have lived together many centuries."

When white soldiers first decided to build the new post that would become Fort Sill near Medicine Bluff just outside the refuge, the Comanches were perplexed by the soldiers' leisure time activities, which included using the bluff as a backstop for target practice. I guess the Comanches felt the same way today's Baptists would feel if a gang of rowdies decided to shoot up the local church. In his book, Meadows points out that "the best known Kiowa geosacred site is Medicine Bluff. It's reported that Comanches used Medicine Bluff and the point of Mount Sheridan for vision questing. Rock cairns on top of the site (Medicine Bluff) and the Kiowa name for it suggest that they used it in a similar fashion, which Kiowa elders confirm."

In their book *The Comanches: Lords of the South Plains,* Ernest Wallace and E. Adamson Hoebel mention that "Medicine Bluff is another place commemorated in name and held in great reverence by the Comanches as being the abode of a powerful, benevolent spirit." It's been said that when the Kiowas first saw the site, they were astonished at seeing a mountain split in two and half of it gone. Legend has it that they referred to the phenomenon as Medicine Split in Two Mountain, and agreed they'd seen nothing like it in their long tribal journey down from the vicinity of the Black Hills.

Geologists say that the 300-foot-tall bluff is composed of rhyolite showing vertical columnar jointing, characteristic of igneous rocks that cool rapidly at or near the surface. They add that the jointing facilitates weathering and erosion. In other words, the harsh Southern Plains weather and the forces of Medicine Creek flowing at the base of the bluff are responsible for the "split in two" effect, although it does resemble a mound that's been chopped in two with a giant machete, and half removed.

In 2010 Towana Spivey, director of the Fort Sill Museum, watched as a group of riders approached the summit of Medicine Bluff, several of them obviously novices at the art of attaching *Homo sapiens* posteriors to the backs of *Equus ferus caballus*—and keeping their anatomy somewhat in place during the process. The riders were Fort Sill officers, the pilgrimage an opportunity to learn about, and actually absorb, some of the culture and history of this place where they'd been stationed by Uncle Sam.

"This is a very important site for many reasons to this area, and it's critical, or almost paramount, to the establishment of the post," Spivey pointed out in a story appearing in the April 8, 2010, *Lawton Constitution*: "It had long been a place to come for sacred ceremonies. We found in little niches along the face of the bluff over a long period of time objects that had been deposited there as offerings."

Spivey added that the offerings ranged from "prehistoric stone chip tools, arrowheads and effigies to more modern artifacts, such as a tin cup, a fork and a spoon." The museum director also found the site of an old sweat lodge, with the entrance facing the high point of the bluff. Normally the entrance to a sweat lodge faces east toward the rising sun. However here, Spivey said, "the bluff is a higher, stronger power."

Commanding officers at Fort Sill generally have been lenient in allowing local Indians to visit and perform ceremonies. Still, it seems both strange and sad that the Southern Plains tribes don't have possession of this, one their most sacred sites, or that the

Medicine Bluffs isn't at least a part of the public domain, or even of the refuge.

The Wichita Mountains have in many ways remained a physical representation of a former way of life practiced over several centuries by Kiowa, Comanche, Kiowa-Apache, Arapaho, and Cheyenne. Anthropologist Alice Marriott, in commentary appearing in the book *Kiowa Ethnogeography* by William C. Meadows and based upon a drive she took with an elderly Kiowa woman, captured the significance of local landforms and their marriage to tribal memory:

"She took the back road, down through Cutthroat Gap and around Saddle Mountain . . . grandmother showed her places as they went along. 'That big bend there, by the river . . . that's where they held the Sun Dance the year I was born. . .'

"On and on. Every little dip, every bend and curve. The spring where they stopped to drink and water the radiator, even the beds of watercress below it, had their histories and their names. It was all alive, this country. (Some) people walked across it that could not see, but Spear Woman could."

Landmarks like the ones found throughout the Wichitas were critical to nomadic people without a written language. Nineteenth-century explorers, seeking information from members of the Southern Plains tribes as they sought to locate the sources of rivers, found that the old men could draw from memory maps in the dirt with their fingertips that were as accurate as if they'd been recorded with instruments.

A white Comanche captive who learned to know the Wichita Mountains region by heart told his "rescuers" that Comanche young men, upon reaching the age of their first raiding expedition, were gathered into a group by their elders and given instruction on how to find their way deep into Mexico. The would-be raiders were seated in a circle, the captive said, while the old men brought out a bag of sticks. Each stick contained notches equaling the number of days the raiders would be on the trail.

After producing the first stick, an old man drew in the dirt a map of the region to be traveled. It included rivers, streams, hills, valleys, ravines, waterholes. When the young men had committed this map to memory, the second stick was produced, a new map drawn, and on to the end of the journey. According to Comanche oral traditional recorded by Meadows in *Kiowa Ethnogeography*, one such raiding party, none of whom were over 19 years of age and none of whom had ever been to Mexico, traveled from a camp on Brady's Creek in West Texas to raid in and around Monterrey, Mexico, without getting lost or seeking additional guidance.

While the Kiowas and Comanches were allies sharing the same territory, the Kiowas oftentimes camped north of the Wichitas, the Comanches to the south. According to Wallace and Hoebel, a single 1834 Comanche village stretched from the Medicine Bluffs north to Chandler Creek, then south to Wolf Creek, an overall distance of some 15 miles. The region in and around the Wichitas, it seems, afforded fuel, good water, and good grazing for both horse herds and buffalo. Soldiers scouting the area made note of these attributes, and 35 years following the discovery of the huge Comanche village, the Army was surveying the same area for a military base.

When the military arrived in 1869, the region including the Wichitas became less of the epicenter of a vast Plains Indian homeland and more the center of operations for a harsh taskmaster charged with turning warring nomads into peaceful farmers. Part of the process involved the destruction of a religion worshipping a God whose voice could be heard from these mountaintops. But traditional ways are slow to erode, and in many instances indigenous spirituality either went underground or morphed with Christianity to create a workable Plains Indian version.

The government process of wringing the Indian out of the younger generations wasn't pretty, and involved strict bans on anything traditional, including language. I know of men living today who, having been raised by their grandparents, grew up speaking only the Comanche tongue. Sadly they were punished at school for carrying on a conversation in the language they were most accustomed to, and as a consequence dropped out of the educational process at an early age. It's amazing that anything from the traditional cultures managed to survive, considering the strength of will determined to quash it. The fact that many managed to retain some of their native ways is a testimonial to the toughness of America's original people. The love they've retained for who they are and for those who came before them is both powerful and inspirational. I think these mountains understand that Spear Woman was right; this land is inseparable from those who gave it names and kept it holy.

Driving to the refuge in mid-August is an exercise in watching cloud shadows and wondering if they'll congeal and turn into a rain cloud. Several of the small towns bordering the Wichitas have large Indian populations, and it's nice to note that some still build open-air brush arbors in their yards or on their property, preferring the shade of oak leaves to a porch as the place to sit, sweat a little, sip a cold drink and dream the deep dreams of a dwindling summer. Within the refuge, tourists are driving slowly, windows up and air-conditioners blasting. They're staring at the buffalo through tinted glass, but then it's August and the afternoon highs have been averaging around one hundred. The car windows are going to stay up no matter how interesting the scenery or the animals staring back from the other side of the visitors' artificially cooled comfort zone. This is summer in Oklahoma, prime-time for air-conditioning.

I've never understood why tourists come here in August. It is hot, humid, and generally miserable. Today is no exception. The hundred-degree mark should be achieved by two in the afternoon. The only respite from the heat is mounds of cumulus clouds cruising overhead, and it's tempting to try to walk along at the pace of a cloud shadow.

Both the animals and the people native to this place have a long history of surviving August on the Southern Plains. Therefore it seems only right that those of us who come here to stare out of our car windows at them shouldn't complain about the heat. My mental orders to myself this morning included taking copious notes and pictures. However with the temperature nearing one hundred, note-taking tends to be futile. My pocket notebook is sweat-soaked and unusable after an hour on the trail.

There's a breeze, but the wind blowing from the southwest feels like flame from a butane torch rather than something that might be considered refreshing. Still, it helps keep the biting flies at bay, so I, like the buffalo, suffer the sunlight rather than retreating into the shade of post oaks and blackjacks, where the little vampires masquerading as overgrown house flies wait for the blood meal needed for reproduction.

Out here under the drifting clouds the prairie has a grand and breezy sweep to it, the billowing grassland definitely ocean-like and, today, somewhat oceanic in color. The little bluestem grasses have taken on an August color scheme, a shade of icy blue that reminds me of the color of a once popular shaving lotion. The blue of the grass is also the color of water melting from glaciers, or maybe closer to the popular "swimming pool blue" down at the YMCA.

The color blends beautifully with the dark green of post oak trees scattered across the distances. If there's a clash of shade or tone, I can't see it. Mother Nature tends to mix her colors without regard for the paint chart at Home Depot. Here we have orange, pink, green, brown, yellow, and several shades of blue—all beautiful, made even more so by the early morning and late evening light that painters and photographers love.

One of several species of liatrus, commonly called gayfeather, is starting to flower on a wide prairie that commonly holds lots of buffalo due to periodic prescribed burns that help maintain robust grassland. The Kiowas and Comanches burned these same meadows for the same reason. Fire invigorated the grass, leaving the new green shoots savored by buffalo. Soon this big meadow will be a landscape of purple and green. Big, green flower buds clinging to a stout stem already show a tint of purple, and soon this liatrus patch will shine under bright sunlight, each plant glowing a deep, rich, almost psychedelic purple and mingling with the emerald grass covering the closely cropped meadow. Pale gray Mississippi kites chase insects overhead, and a huge buffalo bull pants from his prone position in a dusty wallow surrounded by the flowers of August: pale lavender wild petunias or ruellia, dark purple ironweed, a tall, grayish white plant sometimes called late boneset, or *Eupatorium serotinum* in Latin, and the golden tints of the early goldenrods.

August may be the monsoon season in the southwestern mountains of New Mexico and Arizona, but any hope of a water-cooled August afternoon in the Wichitas generally results from weather fronts that rarely reach this far south in the summer. Still, there's always the slight chance of an isolated, heat-induced thunderstorm. Otherwise both the buffalo and I can expect little relief from the heat other than some overnight cooling or the water and shade of small lakes and streams scattered throughout the refuge

As a result, most refuge wildlife tends to congregate near water and become nocturnal. A certain amount of diurnal activity continues, especially along the creek banks. However it's mostly of the lilliputian variety, and those who aren't interested in lifestyles of the insect world might be better served by a trip to a municipal water park or the mall.

By mid-August the streams in Charon's Garden wilderness have grown tepid and sulk in pools, but it's the kind of water dragonflies and damselflies love. And, speaking of love, 'tis the season for aquatic insects to invest strenuously in species renewal, with honeymoons on the wing common around standing water. *Ceratophyllum demersum,* an aquatic plant commonly called hornwort or coontail, grows bank to bank now, supplying oxygen to multitudes of small creatures that escape heat and predators by hiding in the submerged vegetation's shade. A bright red male cardinal leads several recently fledged young on a foraging expedition through the streamside oaks and elms, while several longhorn cattle use their tails to battle flies while feeding on green growth still to be found in some of the narrow valleys.

The stream's largemouth bass, most averaging around 10–12 inches in length, have retreated to the deepest, coolest water to await autumn rains. The pool offers smaller fish, crayfish, and insects on the menu, and at the moment the diminutive yet athletic bass are continually leaping into the air, hoping to snatch a low-flying dragonfly.

And they most certainly have every opportunity to dine on abdomen of dragonfly served sushi-style. The space over the pool seems to vibrate with the multi-winged maneuvers of dragonflies and damselflies, some with clear wings, some with barred wings, some with amber wings, some with ebony wings, some in the process of losing their wings as a fish more determined than the rest rockets into the air and snags a big dragonfly skimmer.

It takes a determined bass to burst through the hornwort and still clear that much air, but the big dragonfly is a tasty morsel, a satisfying mouthful, and the skimmers are legion. Most have powder-blue abdomens and black-barred, clear wings. However time spent on a rock observing the sleepy afternoon's winged side-show reveals reddish amber wings among the mix, plus swarming metallic green damselflies with black wings: ebony jewelwings, *Calopteryx maculata,* one of the more beautiful insects on earth when encountered in streamside-dabbled shade near a small riffle that adds music and motion to the scenery.

Within a few minutes both the shrubbery and my shirt and cap are covered with ebony jewelwings, the damselflies engaged in a more deliberate, fluttering flight than dragonflies, which tend to dart around like helicopter gunships. Both tribes make good use of the streamside switchgrass clumps, which serve as a staging area for an afternoon of territorial patrolling and the occasional nuptial flight.

By mid-month much of the growth on the drier uplands has gone dormant, content to surrender to the heat and wait for more favorable temperatures and rainfall. Both blue and hairy grama grasses atop dry, rocky hummocks have slipped into dull brown inactivity. Fortunately for grazers they maintain nutrients, even in wintertime when the gramas form a sort of standing hay crop. Several short-grass species cure naturally on the stem, retaining enough food value to help buffalo survive at a time when calories are needed.

Even the prickly pear cactus pads appear withered by the August heat. However some of the toughest native prairie plants are flourishing. These include the annual ragweeds, plants that produce an extravagance of seeds relished by ground-nesting birds including bobwhite quail. Ironically, those who curse ragweed for the allergens produced in autumn include hunters who bemoan the demise of what was once the nation's favorite game bird. Bobwhites and other grassland dwellers suffer due to diminished grassland habitat, where natural disturbance allows for the abundant growth of ragweeds. The plant in turn fattens birds that seek the seeds throughout winter. The seasonal sniffles seem a small price to pay when these plants and others cursed and attacked with herbicides contribute so much to the well-being of native wildlife.

Hot, dry weather has resulted in lots of listless-looking trees shedding some of their leaves as photosynthesis shuts down, awaiting cooler weather and a refreshing rain. The trees are far from dead; they're simply suspending everyday operations until the days are more conducive to the business of converting sunlight to usable energy. For now, the system's been overwhelmed by a typical August during this, the sun's dominant season.

Fortunately for the buffalo, water remains available in the form of manmade lakes and ponds plus several small streams. A herd of bulls, cows, and calves, maybe 100 animals in all, have gathered along one of the streams to drink and graze bottomland grasses. One bull takes a break from sucking down water by the gallon in order to scratch his ample undercarriage on a granite boulder, a big rock that's the perfect height for a belly rub. Another bull wades into a pool below a small waterfall to catch the cooling spray tumbling over an extended rock shelf. Refreshed, he samples the flavor of blue leaves extending from a clump of streamside switchgrass.

A buffalo calf watches for a moment, then decides to try a bite from the expansive seed head developing atop the stout, blue-tinted switchgrass stalk. The inflorescence of this sturdy grass is open, airy, and comprised of multiple tiny branches bearing either miniscule flowers or developing seeds. The calf munches as if it's cotton candy, a four-legged kid willing to try anything the adults eat.

After sucking up their fill of creek water, the bulls retire to what comes naturally to males of all species—a nap after lunch. They don't wander far; a meadow bordering the stream is covered with dense and exceedingly blue little bluestem grass. The buffalo are almost hidden when they lie down in this, their summer blue pastures. A few tall, widely scattered post oaks grow near the water, and the cows gather in the shade, seemingly to gossip about the day's events. The ladies keep up a running discourse of grunts and low-pitched, throaty bleats. The resting bulls huff and grumble like old men on a golf course who can't stand the summer heat.

However, the weather's no problem for the calves, who investigate everything that moves, missing little, learning much. After about 30 minutes a grumpy bull, a big guy with a topknot so black it almost appears blue in bright sunlight, rises and confronts another, smaller male that's been grazing at the water's edge. The bigger animal huffs with a sound resembling an old steam engine starting up, then issues a deep bleat that's ignored by the second bull, who appears content to continue his grazing. The contrary bigger fellow, his mood soured by the afternoon sun, stalks around almost stiff legged for a minute or so, then returns to the tallgrass for a belligerent show of dirt pawing, then another nap.

The fruits of summer are beginning to swell in these timbered bottoms. Tiny green acorns are noticeable on the oaks, while nuts the size of my thumb tip adorn pecan trees. They will become fodder feeding elk, deer, squirrels, and a variety of birds as they ripen. Woodpeckers will cache what they can. Squirrels will bury as many as possible. Whitetail deer and elk will munch on the nutritious mast and fatten themselves in preparation for the lean season soon to follow. With this in mind it's easier to suffer the heat. August is a time for all the plant productivity transpiring during spring to slowly ripen. Even the "dog days" of August can be sufferable if we're willing to adapt. Time to pull off my boots, sit in the shade, soak my feet, and let the minnows nibble.

Later in the afternoon my visit to a manmade waterhole spooks a flock of turkeys. They'd been dusting in the shade of some tall oaks and elms bordering the water, leaving a multitude of scratchy signatures plus feathers and droppings in their wake. Moments later a reddish brown, spotted whitetail fawn bursts from the shade of several post oaks and gallops over a small hill littered with big boulders. A swarm of biting flies, voracious members of the *Tabanidae* tribe, makes standing in the shade sheer torture, and I have to wonder how a fawn manages both flies and ticks during the bug season. Maybe winter doesn't seem so bad to creatures prone to attacks by blood-sucking insects.

In the evening I find that seed ticks, the tiny larvae of the deer ticks common in the refuge, have supped on my ankles, leaving a gratuity in the form of tiny red welts and a craven itch I immediately make much worse by vigorous scratching. High-calorie forage may fall into the slim pickings category by January, but at times I think that winter's hunger pangs might be easier to live with than being eaten alive by seed ticks in summer.

One cannot leave the August Wichitas without checking out all the local news that's fit to print—in this case a mud bank covered with a mingling of raccoon and deer tracks. Last night's party must have been a big hit among the nocturnal social scene. Deer came for a drink, raccoons arrived to feel around with their dexterous front feet for frogs, crayfish, and maybe some mussels. Cricket frogs have been active throughout the day around any standing water, and a frog-lined shrinking pool has caught the attention of a kingfisher. The boldly marked bird with stout bill and feathered crest watches from an old, half-rotten tree trunk with a single limb. When a largemouth bass some six inches long makes a leaping pass at a dragonfly, the bird dives off its perch and, with a splash, comes up with supper.

The light has been growing hazy in the north throughout the afternoon, and an hour before dark it seems certain that we're in luck; a cool front has battled through the heat and approaches the mountains, bringing with it a wind shift and a decisive change in the weather. And, when the wind starts to blow from the north, it's halleluiah time in the prairie dog town near where I've parked my truck.

Dog town activity had been as slow as the weather had been hot. But now, with a cool breeze and the temperature dropping accordingly, the pups have erupted with energy. Suddenly they're wrestling, chasing one another, and seemingly exultant. Obviously the prairie dog elders haven't explained that an autumn preview can happen late in August, even when the heat hangs down like Hell turned wrong side up. In an effort to show ample appreciation, one of the pups runs as fast as possible in a tight circle, just like an excited puppy turned loose in a suburban backyard. Finally, after a minute or so of rapid circling, the pup leaps onto a low boulder, sits back, throws both front feet skyward and lets out an exuberant, loud yip. The gods have taken pity on dog town and turned on the air-conditioning. And this pup, being the reverent sort, shows its appreciation.

While the pup yips his thanks, a buffalo bull moseying through the dog town stops to sniff the fresh wind. The massive animal sticks his neck out and rolls back his upper lip, testing one more time for the aroma of a buffalo gal that's willing. A few hundred yards away a herd of maybe 50 cows and calves, excited by the weather change, break into a fast trot, headed in the direction of distant Elk Mountain. Within seconds the calves break into a gallop, cavorting with one another yet never really outdistancing their mothers. The gait is such that some of the older cows have to run to catch back up with the herd. The afternoon is electric, the wind sweet and promising, the scene one that hasn't been seen all that often since the 1870s. For a lingering moment amid this ancient pile of rock, I feel I'm part of a landscape that measures its birthdays by the millions, Something as simple as a storm has pushed back time a measly century and a half. September is coming and with it autumn rains. Once again the landscape is yielding to the timeless dictates of the seasons.

GRAZING ELK. A bull elk and his harem graze the extensive grasslands near wildlife refuge headquarters.

September

Tarantulas are on the move this morning. These large, hairy brown spiders, some with leg spans reaching four inches, most likely have left their burrows to search for female companionship. Males in a mating mindset seek out lady tarantulas in their bachelorette digs, make the appropriate moves to break the ice, and then, after breeding, leave the premises before becoming supper. Female tarantulas generally are larger than males, and, other than a handy snack, have little use for the opposite sex past deposition of sperm. No time for an obligatory post copulation cigarette when tarantula love is in the air. Best to make tracks and live to tell about the conquest, rather than end up consumed by it.

It seems to be a fine day for tarantula amours. According to the weatherman the temperature will struggle to exceed 80 degrees today. The morning has been more like May and soothed by strong south winds. There's a sense that a brutally hot summer is losing its grip, and creatures on the move range from tarantulas to turkeys.

A flock of Rio Grande wild turkeys joins the restless parade. A dozen hens and at least one old long-bearded tom take flight from nearby treetops and land along a stream bordering the wilderness. At the same time a pair of bright orange and black Baltimore orioles busily comb through the foliage of a streamside walnut tree.

Walnuts waste little time turning colors after the fruits are ready for distribution. The refuge is still some two months away from a killing frost, and already the walnut leaves show the yellowish tint of late autumn, prime time advertising employed by nearby sumac shrubs as well. As with all life on the refuge, the business at hand is to pass along genes through progeny. Red leaves on sumac advertise ripening fruit. Seeds will pass through some wild creature's digestive system ready to root and grow, replete with fertilizer. The walnut tree requires a little help from fox squirrels in the refuge woodlands, rodents noted for their willingness to cache food for the winter. Some walnuts will be dug up and consumed during the upcoming months. However a few will be forgotten, sprout into seedlings and, with luck and time, eventually replace the parent trees.

The banks of a small pool churned and muddied by buffalo hooves holds enough water for dozens of leopard frogs. They leap and splash with every step I advance, the majority most likely the offspring of last spring's choristers I listened to near this same spot in late March. The muddy banks also show evidence that raccoons frequent this place on their nightly rounds. Frogs rate high on the favored food list of predators including snakes, raccoons, mink, red-shouldered hawks, herons, egrets, and others with a taste for frog legs, once a culinary mainstay for southern country folk as well. It's doubtful that many of these frogs, assembled for their first full season as part of the refuge fauna, will still be around when it's time to sing for a mate during the upcoming breeding season.

Nature deals with heavy predation by providing prodigious numbers to absorb attrition. Frogs and toads lay thousands of eggs. Yet not all are destined to hatch, nor are all tadpoles that do hatch guaranteed a safe and secure journey to adulthood. Some may be eaten, or die as a gilled juvenile in a dry pool, unable to mature into an air-breathing, land-loving adult frog before the liquid realm of their birthright evaporates. Young leopard frogs that do survive tend to be eagerly sought fare. To compensate, adult breeders must rely on numbers to supply a conduit for their genes. It's a young frog's business to be among the lucky ones, achieve maturity and breed feverishly and as often as possible since after all, the species' future depends on it. Frog survival is a numbers game plain and simple, a system that's remained successful for thousands of years until pollution and habitat destruction became part of the survival equation and numbers began to recede.

The sounds of summer and autumn seem split almost evenly this morning. At first the field crickets graced the granite outcrops with their sweet and lonesome chorus, only to be replaced around 10:30 in the morning by the eardrum-shattering buzz of cicadas, a sound that's more akin to a jackhammer busting cement than an insect love song.

Still, all this racket must contain a few winsome notes appreciated by female cicadas, because the insects certainly aren't in short supply this summer. That's good news to cicada killer wasps. These big, black and yellow specialized predators synchronize their egg-laying efforts with the summer period when calling cicadas are most numerous.

What happens next in the cicada killer/cicada relationship could double as the script of some macabre science fiction movie. Female wasps seek out cicadas and sting them, but only to paralyze, never to kill. Killing will eventually end up as the job of the wasp larvae entombed with the immobile cicada. The female wasp digs a burrow, deposits the paralyzed prey, lays an egg and then seals the earthen chamber that will serve as a nursery for the larva, a wretched tomb for the cicada. The newly hatched wasp begins life with a ready food source, an immobilized cicada faced with the prospects of being eaten alive. Gruesome stuff, maybe, but an efficient and effective way to ensure that, in a couple of weeks, junior reaches adulthood well fed. Strangely enough, the parent wasp that concocts this little chamber of horrors is a vegetarian, dining on flower pollen and sap.

A revived flowering season is underway now that the frying pan heat of July and August has been tempered by shorter days, cooler nights, and an increasingly active weather pattern serving up renewed rainfall. Stout, gray-green stalks of late boneset are wrapped up in tendrils of wild bean, the vines bearing small pink flowers. Knee high goldenrod joins with gumweed and broomweed to paint the prairie distances the smoky gold of approaching autumn. Several orange and black cerambycids, or long-horned flower beetles, have settled onto bright purple Leavenworth's eryngo. These beautiful beetles with their long, graceful antennae feed on pollen provided by this uniquely formed prairie flower that resembles a thistle and adds a contrasting shade of regal color to September's bronze and gold.

On the ninth day of the month, passing thunderstorms immerse the refuge with a refreshing north wind, product of a cool front that keeps the afternoon high from reaching much beyond 80 degrees. This particular September already has witnessed several fronts that triggered thunderstorms and left cooler weather in their wake. As a result some of the spring flowers have staged a second coming, a testimonial to temperature, rainfall, and length of daylight mirroring the April growing season.

Wood sorrel is blooming again in a narrow canyon cooled by a slowly dripping spring, the soft lilac hues of this wildflower with its clover-like leaves complimenting the yellow and white flowers of false garlic, the same odorless member of the lily family that practically covered these same grassy meadows in April. Verbena, another early spring favorite, once again glows neon pink.

It's been a productive growing season, made so by the absence of extended drought. Several whitetail does with fawns in tow have been energized by the cool wind and beneficial summer groceries. They mill around and leap into the air, exhibiting the healthy vitality of good nourishment. None of the fawns shows spotting. They've transcended their baby markings and grown into young adulthood. Now they're big enough to flee on the hoof with their mothers, rather than remain hidden as they did several months ago, depending upon their ability to blend into the background and lack of scent to deter fawn-seeking coyotes hoping to feed young of their own.

A rainy summer and early autumn has left the prairies predominately green. Patches of blue grama grass display little eyebrow-shaped seed clusters atop 12-inch stalks that wave in the wind like tiny flags. Slender bluet damselflies seem to float around streamside vegetation, the males the color of a sky over Santa Fe. At the same time hordes of dragonflies are darting about faster than the eye can follow over open grassland far from water. When I finally get a close look at one they appear to be variegated meadowhawks, late summer and autumn fliers that seem sans flashy colors until examined closely. Under magnification, an intricate pattern of red, yellow, silver, and gold show why female dragonflies of the species are generally smitten by these wild fliers with their gyroscope maneuvers and love of open spaces.

The meadowhawk chase ends near a small damp meadow. At the center grows a single white lily, the flower stalk knee high, the flower itself a singular object of snowy white art. The plant is a rain lily, *Cooperia drummondii*.Rain lilies flower following autumn rains atop a smooth, hollow stem. The flower itself is around two inches in diameter and elegant, a perfect tribute to the end of summer.

A colony of flowers that look like snow from a distance seems to have circling streamside insects enraptured. Up close the "snow bank" turns out to be flowering clammyweed. The flowers have attracted a white-lined sphinx moth, an insect capable of hovering like a hummingbird and extracting nectar with a long, specially evolved proboscis. These moths are so hummingbird-like in flight that they're oftentimes confused with their avian counterparts, especially since many are busily checking out flowers during the daytime.

On the banks of the stream an aging, multi-trunked oak appears mired in confusion. Khaki-colored, male flower tassels dangle from several branches. The weather may seem spring-like, but the tree is more than four months late in its desire to produce an acorn crop. Maybe an earlier attempt failed, or the tree has reacted to length of daylight, temperature, and rainfall reminiscent of the original flowering season. Trees in this region oftentimes rush the flowering and leafing out process due to abnormally warm early spring weather, only to suffer a hard freeze when an eighty-degree day is followed by nights with temperatures in the twenties. Schizoid weather patterns are the norm here rather than an exception, and plants adjust by priming new, tender foliage with an arboreal version of antifreeze. And, if the latent cold is too harsh even for a little homemade antifreeze, the trees turn to auxiliary buds to leaf out again. But this old oak, flowering in autumn, hints at senescence or disease. Maybe it's the tree's last gasp, a final try to get an acorn in the ground and reproduce prior to becoming a smorgasbord for woodpeckers and beetles.

Beneath the oak a barren buffalo trail is at the moment a super highway for a big, black and shiny Bess beetle, an insect family more common in the tropics. However a couple of species are native to the eastern United States, and are often called Betsy bugs by kids drawn to their sleek black elytra and size.

These insects, members of the *Passalidae* family, are not only big but social in an almost human sort of way. Bess beetles share family-rearing duties and also communicate audibly with each other. The beetles feed on rotting wood and, although formidable looking, are essentially harmless. Today the Bess beetle crossing the trail beneath the aging oak is dragging a struggling millipede as if it's on the immediate menu—definitely a non-vegetarian meal and something my reference books fail to explain. The millipede appears to be in its death throes, and the Bess beetle appears to be determined to haul this prize on down the trail. I can't tell if the beetle was the assassin or if it found the millipede and decided to take it home for purposes as yet undisclosed. All I can say for sure is that the inch-and-a-half-long "Betsy bug" is making tracks, and that the prize it carries appears to be something worth fighting for.

Shorter days and cooler nights mean crayfish are active once again during daylight in the streams draining the refuge. Some of the "crawdads" are quite chunky and six inches long or more—a great catch for largemouth bass cruising Panther Creek and enjoying the comfortable water temperatures that return in autumn. However, a slim brown water snake, maybe three feet long, has made the catch of the day. The snake has a leopard frog by the midsection and hangs on determinedly while some six inches of agitated frog struggles frantically to escape. After several minutes of thrashing and splashing the snake manages to drag the frog onto the bank, where the captor prepares to begin the business of unhinging its jaws and swallowing what appears to be the best meal of the summer. Finally the dispirited frog quits fighting and informs the world of its fate through plaintive croaking, the volume diminishing with every croak.

In the heart of Charon's Garden wilderness an afternoon high near eighty coincides perfectly with a light south wind arriving on the heels of a very spring-like shower. A narrow canyon bordered by nearly vertical granite slabs opens into a mini-meadow laced with spring flowers, all showing utter disregard for the regimen of seasons. Some of the milkweeds are once again in flower, and a man without a calendar might be on the lookout for monarch butterflies on the march north from their winter roost in Mexico. In the spring monarchs would be tumbling out of the sky to give these plants enough scrutiny to ascertain their monarch caterpillar growing capabilities. But this is September rather than late April, and at the moment monarchs are drifting south rather than north, waiting for a strong front that will help propel them across the Gulf of Mexico to a winter of semi-torpor in Mexico's evergreen mountains.

At three in the afternoon autumn's official anthem reverberates through a jumble of stacked boulders, each rounded rock as big as an average office building. The sound is amplified inside a narrow slot canyon kept damp and cool by a spring cascading over a series of miniature waterfalls. The flow trickles across erosion-polished granite stairs to be stored in washtub-sized stone basins. Dark green ferns line the canyon walls. They muffle all but the sound of my breathing, and a ton of bull elk's call to arms.

Just a few weeks ago this big guy was grazing peacefully at dusk where the spring flow falls from the granite and empties into a small meadow ringed with post oak trees. But now, due to hormones heightened by declining daylight, he's turned into a morose, foul tempered bully ready to thrash any adversary that answers his challenge or stands in his way. The object of all this male rage on the hoof is, of course, cow elk. The bull, with his newly polished antlers six tines to a side and strength gained in lush summer pastures, is focused on the business of corralling a harem.

Therefore the bugle—actually a long, high-pitched whistle followed by several grunting, jackass-like brays—is both a summons to do battle and a warning to other bulls that trespass or harem pilfering will not be tolerated. Even a long, high whistle on my part, puny though it may be, draws an instant reply. This bull is glued to some shrubby oak thickets on the northern flank of the wilderness, and he's much easier to hear than to see. When I do get a glance it looks as if he's been gardening. Roots, dirt, and vegetation still cling to the bruiser's antlers. The bull is a high octane combination of ardor and anger and, since nothing resembling a rival has stepped forward for a tussle, he's depressurized a bit by battling a streamside embankment and a cedar tree.

Bugling elk conjure images of frosty nights in the northern Rockies, and maybe even a few flurries of early snow. But here in the South the temperature oftentimes climbs close to 100 degrees in September. Therefore randy bull elk find that early morning is best for jousting with a rival or making a date. Even the most belligerent bull may slack off at midday. But let a cold front slip in and bring with it some cool, cloudy weather, and these guys go looking for a fight dawn to dusk. When that optimum day arrives, the bugling that erupts from mountain to canyon to oak grove builds to magnificent opera, a cascade of visceral battle cries speaking to the essence of wild creatures and wild places as clearly as church bells over a monastery.

By the third week of September the heat is back. The afternoon has the look and feel of late June, with contrasting gray and white thunderheads spiraling up both east and west of the refuge. The wind blows out of the south and brings with it moisture from the distant Gulf of Mexico. It appears that the 93-degree heat could trigger a storm.

Previous storms have kept an ample larder of good grazing available in the shaded valleys, and hoofed salad eaters have been busy browsing the tall, winged stalks of a verbesina commonly called frostweed or yellow ironweed. Both leaves and flower stalks look like they've been assaulted by a weedeater, leaving shorn green shoots three to four feet tall. A few plants in this colony managed to escape the scalping with flower buds intact, and will grace the refuge with showy flowers in a day or two.

A jumble of car-sized boulders near the heart of the wilderness area offers escape from the heat and a bed for the second seasonal coming of lavender phlox, the familiar "sweet William" wildflower last seen in early spring. An opening in the boulder field leads to a hidden meadow harboring a small pond approaching the size of the average living room back in suburbia. The pool is grown up in cattails, as well as home to dozens of leopard frogs that abandon the sunny perimeter and dive for the safety provided by a foot or more of murky water. Great blue herons should dine on frog legs late this afternoon—it's apparent that at this wilderness supermarket, the shelves are well stocked.

The heat belies seasonal facts of life cued by the approaching autumn equinox. The red-orange buffalo calves of May are growing winter coats the same brown shade of their elders. Scissor-tailed flycatchers are staging prior to migration in great flocks that weigh down the utility lines where they perch. Occasionally one of the birds darts from the wire, snares an insect out of the air, then returns to its place in the lineup. Before long these birds will be bound for life south of the Equator, in quest of the endless bugfest and a life of acrobatics on the wing.

By evening the gray and white thunderheads have taken on a golden glow, tinted along the edges with streaks of scarlet. Just at sundown the clouds start to swirl and the lightning begins. A hard rain laced with hail follows.

HOME ON THE RANGE. A small bison herd grazes near Quanah Lake. The animals are descendants of several bison donated by the New York Zoological Society in the early 1900s.

October

Where the majority of monarch butterflies went in autumn, and why, was a mystery until 1976. Then, following nearly 40 years of pursuit, Dr. Fred Urquhart revealed in the pages of *National Geographic Magazine* that millions of these insects wintered in the highlands of Mexico's Michoacan. Monarchs reaching their wintering grounds congregate in mountainside trees at elevations around 10,000 feet. Here they remain mostly inactive, protecting fat reserves needed for the spring flight back to the U.S. And, while the Sierra Madre overwintering habitat can be chilly due to elevation, the monarchs compensate by clustering. Tens of thousands may roost in a single fir tree, creating their own self-heated microclimate.

Some of these butterflies travel 3,000 miles or more to reach the Michoacan uplands, with many passing through the Wichita Mountains on their unparalleled autumn flight. The butterflies ride both thermals and the north winds arriving with October cool fronts. Refuge grasslands welcome these intercontinental travelers with flowering sprays of pale purple asters, each spray an excellent refueling station for butterflies that migrate like birds.

Nectar sippers find that October in the Wichitas oftentimes can be a second spring. Days can be cool, nights crisp. Generally rain returns in the form of thunderstorms that echo those in May. Birds are moving, insects mating, and mammals working overtime to put on pounds and grow winter coats. The first hard, killing frost generally won't come until late in the month or sometimes deep into November. For a few weeks, it seems, the land luxuriates in its own redolent splendor, the waning October sun illuminating rich shades of green and gold, butternut and copper. The growing season has reached a seedy climax, and summer's deep green force is preparing to sink slowly back into the soil. It's a thinner light that shines now, warming days of uncommon clarity and rarified air.

Charon's Garden contains an imposing old post oak with a broad trunk wrapped in a garland of the climbing vine known as woodbine. The vine's tendrils cling to numerous footholds in the dark and gnarly bark, and bright scarlet leaves advertise the ripeness of blue-black woodbine fruit. By the second week in October this tenacious vine has finished its work for the season. Soon the brilliant red leaves will disperse on a strong south wind that still smells faintly of summer.

The old post oak host tree, on the other hand, remains stubborn. Green leaves are still in place, even though many are weather-ravaged and insect-chewed. In fact the entire tree seems somewhat disheveled due to all the damage the oak has endured throughout the growing season. The aged tree has battled insect onslaughts and infestations with chemical compounds drawn from the soil by the roots and then mixed in a formula of the tree's own making. This old oak can't flee insect attack or visit the pharmacy, so over thousands of years it and its tribe have perfected a potent underground laboratory of oak homeland security, brewing insecticides delivered within the oak's own sap. Still, in the end, a few months' rest won't hurt this patriarch tree shading a piece of autumn-bronzed meadow. The tree's only winter task will entail providing a stout, scratchy surface for buffalo to rub away at lingering itchiness. The bison will polish the bark to a near glasslike sheen in the process, and maybe a coyote will ramble by to hike a leg and leave a song dog version of a mass email.

The warmth of the afternoon has created thermals, or updrafts, and migrating hawks circle overhead, riding these air currents higher and higher. Most likely it's a flock of Swainson's hawks, drifting their way back to wintering grounds in South America. By midwinter these raptors will siesta in warmer latitudes while mountain bluebirds from New Mexico flock into the southwestern Oklahoma prairies, announcing their arrival with a flash of turquoise on the wing. For refuge buffalo, moving with the seasons is no longer an option. High fences have put a stop to long-distance migration. Therefore they grow winter coats and pack on as many pounds as possible, surviving as an animal that, blessed with good health and allowed ample forage, remains well equipped to endure any upcoming hard weather.

In many ways October is as near to perfection as life gets here on the weather-challenged Southern Plains. The heat of summer has faded, January's chill is still months away. October rains refresh the grass, refill the streams, and bring wildflowers back for an encore. Buffalo are active in October, with calves bucking and playing behind cows constantly in search of the last, best green grass. The bulls luxuriate in the sun and offer grunting praises to a season refreshed by cooling breezes. For a while at least, life will be lived mostly sans strife as the big guys take it easy and anticipate next summer's breeding season.

On the third day of October, sunup illuminates an especially chilly morning. The overnight temperature has dropped into the thirties, and the radio reports an unusually early frost in the state's northeastern counties. The cold is enough to invigorate the refuge's crows, and they're not shy about voicing their attitudes about the upcoming winter. Crickets tune up as the day warms, and islands of

Maximilian sunflowers, growing in mini-groves amid the autumn orange, pink, and bronze stems of bluestem grasses, seem radiantly yellow in the crisp, high pressure light.

A young buffalo bull has become separated from his fellow bison by a woven wire fence. A gap in the fence maybe 100 yards away allowed the bulk of the herd to pass through and begin grazing on broad pastures bordering the refuge's interior mountains. Somehow the young bull missed his fellow's exodus as well as their route. Now he's determined to rejoin his comrades and, even though easy access awaits if the distraught bison would simply seek it out, the massive youngster is determined to "bull" his way through an unyielding manmade obstacle.

The bison's agitation swells as he paces the fence, pawing and raking at the ground with hooves and horns, tossing both dirt clods and grass overhead and onto his hump, basically letting the world know he's not happy. Soon the pacing picks up speed and the bison mutters a few grunting oaths as only a perplexed buffalo can. Hopefully the pacing and lamenting will subside around nap time, and the situation won't seem so desperate. I give the animal a wide berth, and by mid-afternoon he's discovered the gap in the fence and returned to resting peacefully with his buddies.

Another buffalo bull grazing with a small bachelor herd wears a wooly topknot crowned with cockleburs. Massive as the animal is, he looks a bit clownish as clouds gather south and west, and the late afternoon sun peers through holes in the gathering gray shroud. One brilliant shaft of light illuminates the scarlet leaves of a sumac patch growing next to this magnificent bison and his crown of thorns. For a few minutes the dramatically lit bull atop the rocky knoll seems to be starring in a Cecil B. DeMille biblical extravaganza. The great beam of sunlight reflects both the buffalo's cocklebur headdress and adjacent crimson leaves, presenting a scene that would be artistically appropriate for the Easter sunrise services held each spring on this refuge.

The following morning this same section of the refuge plays host to a wildlife show that would gladden the heart of any documentary filmmaker. A sunrise with temperatures in the low fifties merges into a midday nearing seventy. Flocks of sandhill cranes migrate overhead, and their trembling whinny echoes an ancient voice that resonates perfectly with these aged granite ridges. An osprey leaves a small lake reluctantly, its mournful keening directed at the two-legged interloper who has arrived to interrupt the bird's fishing. Several young bull elk graze in bright sunlight, while a few hundred yards beyond, a rugged looking old bull herds more than a dozen cow elk, his hard-to-confine October harem.

Buffalo nose through a ragweed patch to find the nutritious grama grass concealed there. The ragweeds, pale gray-green, now dominate on spring burns that have been repeatedly and closely cropped by both longhorns and buffalo. Next year the prescribed burns will be set in some other part of the refuge, this patch will rest, and the perennial grass roots will eventually outcompete the annuals. In the meantime, the nutritious weed seeds will serve as critical winter fodder for quail and meadowlarks.

Dew is heavy on the refuge's granite outcrops on a foggy morning midway through the month, and a wan sun peeling back the overcast allows the rock to shine like polished chrome. A screech owl whinnies from somewhere in the middle of an oak grove, the sound otherworldly in this sea of landlocked cloudiness.

It's the kind of morning that brings elk out of the oak groves and onto the meadows, and several can be seen grazing in the open when the sunlight finally grows strong enough to reveal them. For a while the fog hangs in the valleys and swirls around the mountains like a bright silver spider wrapping up its prey. Autumn colors, intensifying and waning as the sunlight ebbs and flows, range from the silver pink of glistening seeds on a clump of lovegrass to the rich reds and oranges of fog-bound bluestem. In the background the oaks seem almost black, except for a patchwork quilt of rich scarlet mottling scrambled throughout the otherwise green leaves.

A walk back into the wilderness area startles a bull elk and sends him crashing through the oak scrub at a gallop. And, while this big fellow disappears into the fog, other bulls are piercing the sky's low ceiling with their battle cries. When a bull on the ridgeline bugles, another in a meadow just a few yards away from where I'm standing issues a ringing reply. Both remain lost in the fog, and I'm able to stay unseen in the midst of this savage philharmonic, all the time occupying the best seat in the house. As long as I'm quiet and stationary, the challenges continue.

The sky clears around noon, and the elk retire from threats of mortal combat to more urgent necessities like sleep, food, and water. The elks' autumn anthem is replaced by quarrelsome bluejays, the birds remarkably shrill if not so wildly musical as the elk. Swarms of harvestmen spiders, the "granddaddy long legs" that have fascinated country children for centuries, have massed on granite boulders and await afternoon heating that will radiate from the rock. A pair of bright red dragonflies remain coupled on the wing, and the assembly call of bobwhite quail pierces the stillness just a few minutes after I flush at least a dozen of the handsomely attired little grassland dwellers. Bright orange comma butterflies sweep past, attracted by a wide palette of autumn wildflowers: purple liatrus, blue-flowered autumn onion, ubiquitous clumps of both lavender and white asters, bright yellow broomweed, and burnished sprays of goldenrod. A butterfly would do well to be on the wing and active on a day like this, one in which the afternoon high approaches a perfect 72 degrees. The wind remains light and life on the plains remains rejuvenated and restive.

October 18 is an important date in the Wichitas. On this day, in 1907, America began the process of bringing back the buffalo by releasing 15 animals on this, their original national refuge.

The Wichitas became the nation's first buffalo refuge due to circumstances stretching back to 1867, when Congress set aside much of southwest Oklahoma, then Indian Territory, as a reservation for the Kiowa, Comanche, and Kiowa-Apache. The reservation encompassed the Wichita range and included land between the Washita River and the Red, the latter delineating the northern border of Texas.

The tribes were finally subdued by the military, with the last holdouts rounded up and resettled on the reservation by the early 1870s. Soon market hunters were swarming over the buffalo country these tribes had been forced to abandon. The commercial killers found they could make a profit by stripping the hides from the remaining herds and selling them to be made into industrial belting.

Due to the efficient efforts of the hide men, the American bison or buffalo was virtually extinct by the turn of the century, except for those protected in Yellowstone National Park and animals captured and kept on private ranches. At the time bison were reintroduced onto the Southern Plains, only an estimated 2,000 animals were still scattered across the continent.

The Kiowa, Comanche and Kiowa-Apache and their descendants had been told, at the time of their final treaty, that the reservation in southwest Oklahoma was theirs forever. But when land available for settlement grew scarce elsewhere, lawmakers, speculators, and land hungry farmers and ranchers pressured Congress and the president to open Indian Territory reservations to white settlement.

The effort to enact this land grab was intense, and President William McKinley capitulated in 1901, instructing Congress to draw up plans to grant each tribal member a small individual allotment and then open the rest of the reservation to the public. And, while McKinley was mulling over the fate of the Kiowa–Comanche–Kiowa-Apache homeland, territorial businessmen who'd already settled in what was to become Oklahoma were petitioning the president and Congress to have the Wichita Mountains held out of the land grab. Instead they wanted the mountains protected as a national park.

Influential Oklahomans including the heads of various civic groups approached Vice President Theodore Roosevelt with a plan. Roosevelt, in Oklahoma City in 1900 to attend a reunion of the Rough Riders, a cavalry unit he recruited and led into battle in the Spanish-American War, was known for his conservation sentiments. The locals argued for a national park in the Wichitas, while Roosevelt envisioned the mountains as a perfect place to restore the buffalo to their rightful home. Unfortunately, when Congress adjourned in 1901, all thoughts of the new national park rode the rails home with them.

The slight, however, didn't deter Oklahoma Territorial Governor William Jenkins. While in Washington D.C. to work on a plan for opening the reservation to settlement, Jenkins pressed the president to protect the Wichita Mountains. McKinley finally agreed to set aside the Wichitas' scenic core as a national forest preserve. This was a safe political gesture, because McKinley had been told the mountains were virtually worthless for any commercial venue other than tourism.

The Wichitas were too rocky to plow, but easy on the eyes in a region where the view was mostly grass and sky. In essence, the area's scenery saved it. Oklahomans continued to clamor for national park status. But for McKinley, keeping settlers out of the core area was enough of a favor. In time the push for a park faded, and with it any effort to upgrade the region's public identity by establishing a national park.

The presidential forest preserve proclamation kept land seekers at bay, but did little to stop hunters from exploiting the game rich mountain range. When Teddy Roosevelt succeeded McKinley, he did what he could to stop the slaughter by turning the Wichita forest preserve into a national game preserve. Sadly, by this time there wasn't much left to protect. The war on predators continued, resulting in the extermination of the last wolves and bears.

Newly inaugurated President Roosevelt never forgot his desire to return the bison to the plains. In 1905 a member of the New York Zoological Society surveyed the Wichitas to see if the area was appropriate for bison restoration. Roosevelt had informed Congress that the refuge would be a great area to bring back the buffalo, and William T. Hornaday, president of the recently formed American Bison Society, joined the push to make the Wichitas the nation's first national bison refuge.

Hornaday solicited funds to purchase bison from the remaining private herds. The animals were cared for at the New York Zoological Park, predecessor of the Bronx Zoo. In March 1905, the New York Zoological Society told Congress they'd donate several animals if the government would cover the expense of fencing and maintenance. Congress approved the Wichita Mountains as the release site and appropriated $15,000 for the buffalos' care.

In October of 1907, 15 bison selected from four distinct herds and bloodlines were padded and crated like fine racehorses, each animal carefully readied for what would be a long, rough ride. The animals faced a seven-day train trip stretching from New York City to Cache, Oklahoma—a town barely more than a few frame houses rising from the prairie, but gateway to the refuge at the time.

According to reporters accompanying the train, crowds gathered at every stop to witness the homecoming. Citizens of Cache felt a particular pride in being headquarters to the nation's first buffalo refuge. On October 18, after a 1,858-mile journey, the bison were unloaded from railroad cars and transferred to caged wagons for the final few miles. Reporters wrote that for local Indians, the arrival was more of a spiritual and cultural event than an endangered species restoration effort. Newspapers said many Comanches arrived in their finest tribal attire to welcome home the "Great Spirit's cattle."

Older Indians gathered youngsters to see the animal that, only a few years ago, had symbolized one of the most colorful and free lifestyles on the planet. They told hunting stories and explained how the buffalo had been vital to tribal culture and identity. The Indians formed an entourage as the buffalo, named for famous Plains Indian warriors including Quanah, Lone Wolf, Black Dog, and Geronimo, took a rickety 13-mile ride to a newly fenced 8,000 acre pasture in the heart of the refuge.

The efforts of Hornaday and the New Zoological Society played a huge role in the return of bison to the landscape where their predecessors had prospered like no other animal on the North American continent. But the heart and soul of the bison restoration movement was the man whose energies and ambitions knew few boundaries, and whose love of wildlife and wild places sparked the greatest conservation achievements in the history of the world.

Theodore Roosevelt was an avid hunter, an excellent naturalist, and a man committed to protecting wild areas for future generations. He, along with Hornaday, was instrumental in the formation of the American Bison Society. He'd hunted buffalo from his ranch in North Dakota, and one can only deduce that Roosevelt, along with the plains Indians, mourned the animals' passing.

Theodore, or Teddy to his friends, was also a fan of the Wichita Mountains. One of his Rough Riders had been from the area, and Comanche Chief Quanah Parker was another of the president's favorites.

Quanah had ridden in Roosevelt's inaugural parade, and according to legend Parker had shared with Roosevelt the Kiowa tale about the last buffalo herd retreating into a mystical sanctuary hidden deep within the Wichitas' Mount Scott, where they'd find safety from total extermination. As the story goes, a Kiowa woman down by a stream early in the morning had watched as the mountain opened up and the remaining few buffalo filed in. According to the eyewitness, the prairies gleaming from within the mountain had been lush and green, and the downtrodden animals were eager to make their exodus.

It's possible that Roosevelt hoped to give the legend credence by being instrumental in the buffalo's rebirth here in the shadow of Mount Scott. And, in many ways, the return of the buffalo felt like prophecy. Several among the original New York brood stock had been purchased from Texas Panhandle rancher Charles Goodnight, a former Texas Ranger who turned to ranching when he ended his law enforcement career. Goodnight, at the urging of his wife, captured several animals from the southern herd when it became obvious that few would survive the hide hunters.

In time Goodnight became friends with Quanah Parker, who had called the vast Goodnight holdings home before he and his band were forced onto the reservation by the cavalry. Stranger still was the fact that Goodnight had been among the Ranger contingent that in 1860 attacked Quanah's village along the Pease River near present-day Vernon, Texas. During that raid the Rangers recaptured Parker's mother, who had been taken as a child from a Texas settlement. The young white woman grew up to be 100 percent Comanche in spirit if not in pedigree, and married Peta Nocona, a noted warrior and Quanah's father. When Cynthia Ann and her daughter Prairie Flower were returned to the Texas Parkers, the former captive grieved for her Comanche family and begged to be returned to the plains.

Quanah adopted the Parker name after moving to the reservation and morphed into an astute businessman and leader. He arranged to lease the grazing rights to some 300,000 reservation acres to Texas cattlemen in an effort to generate tribal income. In turn the Texans built Quanah and his wives a spacious, modern house not far from Cache. Roosevelt would be among many powerful figures who dined with Quanah at his "Star House," named for the large stars decorating the roof. There's little doubt that Roosevelt, at the time quickly becoming the most powerful man in America, discussed the possibilities of returning bison to the Wichitas. Certainly it must have been part of the conversation when President Roosevelt arrived in southwest Oklahoma to chase "wolves" (mostly coyotes) with Jack Abernathy, a cowboy legendary for his method of catching the animals by hand.

Quanah and several ranchers were among the entourage following Abernathy and Roosevelt as they rode down coyotes on the open prairie. Later in the trip the president had an opportunity to check out the refuge he'd created. It's not difficult to imagine Roosevelt's toothy smile and the rousing "bully" escaping his lips when he took in the wild scenery and the excellent grassland growing between the granite outcrops. Later, when he pressed Congress to appropriate funds to reestablish bison in the Wichitas, Roosevelt knew from first-hand experience that he'd chosen their home well.

Some estimates place those in attendance at nearly one thousand when the buffalo arrived in Cache. Among the many Indians on hand was Quanah. It's been said that Quanah was one of the individuals who helped unload the animals from their rail cars and reload them in awaiting wagons. According to legend the chief poked the buffalo in the ribs several times, just to make sure he wasn't dreaming.

Before leaving the White House, President Roosevelt added 3,680 additional acres to the refuge. The buffalo herd prospered, grew, and today some 600 animals roam the refuge in comparative freedom, the animals' genetic roots deeply embedded in some of the most turbulent years of western expansion. There are no monuments to Roosevelt and Hornaday within the refuge, but Quanah fared better. He has a namesake lake and stream, probably a more fitting memorial for a man born under the stars. Plus all these buffalo grazing free in a wild setting should be memorial enough for all three men.

It's mid-October and recent rains have left water standing in weathered granite basins and trickling from cracks in the rock. In the distance, both the pothole pools and the silvery patterns in the elevated granite—liquid drawn through solid due to the unique physics of capillary action—glisten in the early morning sun. The day dawns at 60 degrees and the refuge smells like onions. This potent, late flowering variety seems especially aromatic. The flowers are a showy purple, much more so than those that flowered in spring.

We've climbed up the north flank of Elk Mountain, an ascent punctuated with breaks to catch breath and watch season-defying butterflies visit asters bearing dark purple flowers. Atop the mountain, a simple little ladies tresses orchid blooms in a pocket of soil amid granite bedrock covering most of the summit like expensive imported flooring. The yellowish white flowers spin around the orchid's stem like candy striping. The clatter of loose rocks draws my attention to a randy bull elk attempting to block the flight of a cow elk that, at the moment, would rather be elsewhere. Gray moths floating down like cottonwood fluff concentrate around the ubiquitous asters, while collared lizards climb onto rocky outcrops to soak up the season's lingering rays.

After the sun goes down, photographer Don House and I sit next to a fire embellished with glowing cedar coals, the wood cut, cured, and saved for the occasion. The flame burns brightly in bursts of red and blue. In the distance a single coyote's howl ignites a chorus that, in time, circles the campground. The coyotes provide the perfect music for a clear night, stars overseeing a chill predicted to drop into the thirties. Later a screech owl's eerie, high-pitched vibrato motivates a great horned owl to reply in a more subdued basso, each questioning call answered by another and another until the entire oak woods reverberates with these, the most otherworldly of bird calls. Around midnight I'm awakened by snorting, plus the click of unshod hooves. Buffalo wander through the campground within a few feet of my head. At sunrise the alarm clock consists of a covey of bobwhite quail telling the universe that they've survived to sing another day.

A few hours after sunup a group of flickers argue in a dead oak tree, their constant "wicka-wicka-wicka" chatter both loud and agitated. The birds are the yellow-shafted phase. Oftentimes red-shafted flickers are seen in the refuge, as well as those that appear to be orange, probably hybrids here where the range of the western red-shafted and eastern yellow-shafted merge. A walk down the bottom of Quanah Creek flushes a beautiful whitetail buck, a big fellow with four massive tines per antler and a muscular body that should weigh close to 200 pounds. The buck's gathered three does, and a distant bugle by a bull elk sounds as if he wishes he could be so lucky. Big bluestem grass growing in the narrow creek bottom is seven feet or more tall, and I slide into the grass like a child entering a cornfield and slip out of sight. The post oaks growing in the bottom have produced a bumper crop of unusually big, sweet acorns, many of them now on the ground amid neon yellow Maximilian sunflowers mixed with blue salvia the color of the summer sky.

By mid-morning a band of cow elk munches post oak acorns on a ridge near Styx Canyon in the westernmost reaches of the wilderness area. Other than the wind and some occasional bird calls, the predominant sound is crunching acorns with a background of bugling bulls. Some of the buglers can be seen wandering around in the distance, all atop a high ridge of granite extending from Treasure Lake to the western refuge fence. However the cows seemed unconcerned, apparently much more interested in the acorns.

When one of the cows finally sees me she starts up a high-pitched, squealing alarm call that continues for at least 10 minutes. The cow accents her warning by including some stiff-legged dancing in place. In time the cow, less than 30 yards away, wearies of her snorting and strutting and eases away to find another oak laden with ripe acorns as her friends fall in behind.

On the way into Styx Canyon it seems appropriate to stop for a moment and pay homage to the aged buffalo bull that's chosen the boulder ringed meadow on the north rim for his retirement home and final resting place. He's been there since I discovered the nearby rattlesnake den in late March, and seems in relatively good condition. However there's an excellent chance that this winter will be his last, and that I'll find bleached white bones rather than a ton of breathing bison flesh when the meadow greens six months from now.

A waterfall bounces over stair-stepping granite into a pool shaded by tall trees growing near the head of the canyon. Among the big oaks are persimmon trees laden with orange fruit. Deer, coyotes, and raccoons will make quick work of this nutritious bounty as it ripens following a hard frost, and the big seeds will be evident in scat scattered across the refuge.

A brightly sunlit afternoon illuminates wine-colored stalks of big bluestem grass pressed against granite boulders decorated with striking yellow lichen. Closely cropped patches in several grassy meadows bear three awn grass bleached nearly white. The sharply pointed seeds stick in my bootlaces as designed and therefore are off to see the world—or at least a different part of the refuge. It's a cleverly evolved way to colonize new territory. The seeds lodge in animals' coats, eventually rub off or fall out, and, if lucky, land in a spot conducive to growing annual grasses. The success ratio seems excellent, considering the amount of three awn turning winter white here in late October.

A yearling whitetail buck, flushed from a tall stand of Indian grass, sports a single antler, a forkless spike maybe a foot long. The one antler suggests an injury to the missing appendage at some point early in its development. The youngster looks imbalanced, also a bit comical. And maybe it's for the best. He's far too callow to compete for a lady friend, although his hormones tell him otherwise. The Indian grass swale the one-horned buck bolted from is both tall and thick, beneficiary of ample rains through spring and summer. As a result the grasses have grown so dense they're difficult to walk through, yet provide perfect cover for a young deer needing to rest his antler.

Indian grass seed plumes ripen to a beautiful old gold color in October, the color of gold bullion left too long in a sea chest and in need of polishing. An Indian grass lowland, in late evening light, almost seems paved with precious metal. A visitor to the refuge won't find streets paved with gold, but buffalo trails provide the next best thing. All the scene needs is a hymn to make it seem heavenly.

In October even the grasshoppers tend to reflect the color of the sun. One that I find, an especially large specimen, is a bright banana yellow. This fellow's curtain call is still weeks away with the onset of cold weather. But for now, it's eat, mate, and lay eggs—if you're not eaten first, that is, by grassland birds eager for a little autumn protein.

There's a large mesa near the center of Charon's Garden that's especially flat. The summit is a wildlife magnet of sorts, judging by the variety and number of tracks around a manmade pond providing a perfect place to sit and take in the view. Most of the Garden's phantasmagoric rock formations are visible from here, and several small streams drain down and out of sight into some of the most rugged canyons in the refuge. On a morning late in October, following a cool sunrise with a light frost, the sun rises over the lip of the mesa to brighten white asters, blue dayflowers, and gray sagewort bedecked with tiny yellow flowers. Sagewort has a fragrance that's more than medicinal. In many ways it's the most intoxicating scent of the Southern Plains, a balm to remind solitary hikers of a land where buffalo still roam, a place where elk bugle from belly-deep autumn grasses.

October atop the mesa is colorful in the way ancient Indian pottery is colorful: subtle, rich in earth tones that merge to create new tones and shades without delineation or effort. On some mornings the colors and the rich smell of it all is simply delicious. It's as if autumn's final life surge has overwhelmed the senses. October in the Wichitas is a sensual cacophony of natural survival—eggs laid, cocoons spun, hibernation, migration, life retreating underground to return with the sun next spring. The crows down in the canyon have changed their tune from summer raucous to the somber vocabulary of November. The mountains have shrugged away another season, and a canyon wren sings of change.

CEDAR & STONE. A twisted old cedar provides the refuge backcountry with native statuary to match endless acres of sculpture in stone.

November

According to legend, Spanish explorers were in the Wichitas, known then as the Sierra Jumanos, as early as the 1600s, searching for gold. The same legends have it that lost treasure is scattered throughout this jumbled granite uplift. My guess would be that the gold in question, and maybe the impetus for all that misguided searching, is the way the rocks and pebbles at the bottom of November streams glow like manmade jewelry. The clarity of both water and light, coupled with the angle of the sun's rays, make streams here seem paved with gold at times. Maybe that's what some of the Indians were alluding to when they told Coronado that gold was plentiful in their homeland. If so, it was a communications error that brought about torture, terror, slavery, and loss of life and limb for tribal people who couldn't grasp the lust for precious metals driving the invaders. The natives found out about Old World cruelty the hard way when the Spanish discovered that the "golden cities" they'd been seeking were only dusty villages comprised of grass huts.

In time there were people of Spanish descent who learned to both understand and appreciate this oftentimes parched and weathered land, as well as the natives who called it home. Comancheros from north-central New Mexico are known to have traveled to the

Wichitas to trade with Indians of the region. These traders were simple rural people who bartered for buffalo robes by exchanging trinkets and hard bread they baked especially for this enterprise. According to frontiersmen there to witness it, excitement swept through the Indian villages when creaking wooden carts driven by sun-seared men in conical sombreros came into view.

Josiah Gregg, a frequent traveler on the Santa Fe Trail and author of *Commerce of the Prairies* published in 1844, said the Comancheros were "composed of the indigent and rude classes of the frontier villages, who collect together several times a year and launch upon the plains with a few trinkets and trumperies of all kinds, and perhaps a bag of bread or pinole (flour made of ground acorns, mixed with herbs and seeds)."

These New Mexicans were of Hispanic blood, oftentimes mixed with that of one of the Pueblo tribes living along the Rio Grande. They wandered widely in search of trading partners (most often Comanches, thus the name). Comancheros followed trails through the plains connecting precious yet hard to find waterholes, routes known only to them and their Southern Plains customers.

On a November day like today in the Wichitas—low overcast, sharp north wind, steady drizzle—it's easy to sit back against a boulder and daydream about the men in carts carved from cottonwood logs traveling hundreds of miles with little more than the clothes on their backs and maybe some sheet iron perfect for making arrowheads. At times I'm sure drought dried the waterholes and storms threatened the lives of these simple merchants. Still, they knew the land intimately, had learned how to live with it, and existed contentedly on the basis of this knowledge. Such associations—simple and enduring—disappeared with the Comancheros and their Plains Indian allies. Sadly, respect for the Southern Plains landscape, along with the sort of knowledge that preserves land health and thus the health of those living upon it, disappeared at about the same time.

November in the Wichitas is oftentimes a gray month, the melancholy at the end of the growing season, a period when thoughts broadcast widely during spring and summer turn inward upon themselves, to be ruminated like a wad of grass. For those of us who love the land and worry about its future, this month of transition is a time for mulling over environmental paradoxes, for adjusting to the short days and long nights of winters that are generally mild but can turn bitter. At times in November these mountains erupt in beauty that almost seems to explode, as if the fire of life has erupted in a final bright and perfect flame.

By the second or third week of November colors are richer, the days crisper, the wildflower season's final chapter among the most radiant of the year. Animals are active, streams flow again, even the granite seems to take on an inner glow. It's a good time to be alive, even as the life force is receding. The old buffalo bulls stake out their solitary meadows and watch the days unfold, dreaming dreams that remain unknown, observing an annual ritual reaching back to the time of the last continental ice, when people armed with spears arrived to hunt them in packs, like the wolves.

Autumn can be a rainy time in the Wichitas, and on the second day of this particular November, recent rains have turned mountain flanks into waterfalls. Some drop 40 feet or more, bouncing from granite shelf-to-shelf, as beautiful as any in the Rockies. . . but only for a day.

Several whitetail does in a nearby meadow, somber in their thick gray winter coats, stand and stare as the water cascades behind them, a calendar pose as deceiving as it is spectacular. Waterfalls here generally don't erupt into white foam like those in Colorado.

Here they trickle, if they run at all. Except, that is, during the hours after a hard rain. Then they bound from rock to rock as if transplanted from Yosemite.

At midday, scattered boulders beside the waterfalls wear wreaths of yellow asters and green ferns. Towhees scratch for insects in the newly fallen leaves under the oaks, while a striped skunk, rummaging carelessly in the open, smug in the knowledge of its own eye-searing, stinking self defense, noses through green and yellow post oak acorns in search of a fat beetle for lunch. The oaks' bounty is a seasonal magnet for deer, and the does watch my retreat warily, each anxious to return to what a whitetail must regard as true manna from heaven.

Late in the afternoon I stop to watch one of the refuge's best fishermen, a belted kingfisher, dive from a limb into clear lake water and surface with a small sunfish. A pair of pied-billed grebes paddles to the center of the small lake and then disappears like tiny submarines, scanning the depths for a supper replete with scales. In the distance a very dark and ominous-looking cloudbank settles onto the western horizon just at sunset. Then, as a long shadow spreads over the land, the sun seems to explode from below the clouds just before it slips over the edge of the earth. For a moment the mountains are lit up like movie stage props, and the red in the oaks seems to catch fire. Then it all fades into surreal silence, except for the sound of my footsteps on newly fallen leaves.

Although photographers tend to swarm the refuge weekends, one rarely sees a painter perched behind canvas and easel, not an uncommon sight in other parks and refuges. And that's an overlooked opportunity for the artistically inclined, because the Wichitas tempt the palette with both form and color, especially in November.

Photographers here are generally gathering snapshots of prairie dogs and buffalo, taken from the shoulders of refuge roadways. Yet few scenes are more naturally beautiful than the vivid scarlet shades of November sumac growing amid rugged little islands of black rock, or orange boulders stained yellow by lichens and providing a perch for rust-red canyon wrens. Scenes here beg for artistic application of watercolor or oil, a rewarding creative undertaking unless the wind relocates paints and easel to somewhere in the vicinity of Kansas. Creativity on the Southern Plains tends to be more rewarding when practiced in the vicinity of a windbreak, and if the artist's vanity extends to personal grooming, I'd suggest plenty of hairspray.

Bands of autumn color ascending distant Mount Sheridan remind that November is both a migration month and a traditional hunters' moon. The whitetail deer rut happens in November, and hunters outside the refuge are starting to palpitate in anticipation. The rut, or breeding season, means bucks are moving more in the daytime in search of does. At the same time hunters are actively pursuing the bucks pursuing the does. It helps that the search for a lady friend tends to overwhelm normal whitetail deer caution.

Early in the morning on the seventh day of November, the refuge's four-legged suitors are already on the prowl. But hunters here today are only those of us armed with cameras. It's a perfect day for whitetail love: a light north wind, faint white streaks of high cirrus clouds, a high in the low seventies. Not far from the highway a young buck is trailing after a doe that seems in no hurry to be caught. The buck's rather spindly antlers, three forks to a side, suggest that his second birthday will occur sometime in early May or late June of the following spring.

However, his lack of experience has done little to temper either eagerness or ardor. The buck closes on the doe, and for a minute it appears that the deer's love life may be looking up. Then the neighborhood bully eases out of the oaks, and the younger buck suddenly stiffens.

The newcomer appears to be in the prime of life, heavier than the competition, antlers with stout beams and massive bases, plus the self-assurance of a veteran. The big buck sizes up the situation, advances towards the younger deer, then suddenly charges.

The young guy doesn't even bother to bluff. He turns tail and gallops for cover, while the bruiser stops to sniff, obviously certain his competition won't have a courageous change of heart. A few seconds later the heavyweight newcomer is trailing after the doe and the young deer has completely vacated the premises, unaware his hasty retreat has been recorded by mini cams through automobile windows. The older buck and star of this wild kingdom soap opera should have stopped for a moment to thank his proverbial lucky stars for wildlife refuges. Had it been hunters other than tourists, those massive antlers would have become a conversation piece on a den wall, somewhere in suburbia.

Turkey feathers along a little creek tucked away in wilderness granite speaks to the real bird of Thanksgiving—a long, slim, wary wild creature far removed from the fat, white, waddling birds that grace Thanksgiving platters across America. Commercially raised turkeys have little in common with the lean, muscular birds that shed a few feathers beside this stream. Truly wild turkeys like these in the refuge are sharp-eyed and attuned to their surroundings. Those found in supermarkets are barely capable of feeding themselves, the wild genes long ago erased, replaced with body chemistry that prospers under confinement in close quarters.

A boulder the size of a doghouse near the edge of a prairie dog town serves as a perch for a refuge visitor I don't recognize at first. The migrant shows inconspicuous feathering in shades of gray, black, and brown, totally unlike the dapper, tuxedo-like black and white breeding plumage that seems so flashy on the bird's high plains breeding grounds. The lark bunting, now without need for such fancy trappings, has arrived incognito, content to blend into the surroundings and survive a shorter, warmer winter here at the southern edge of its grassy homeland. The winged migrant joins flocks of Iowans and Minnesotans fleeing south on the nearby interstate, the mechanized migrants exercising plans to roost in some trailer park along the Texas coast.

Now that their thick, dark winter coats are in place, the buffalo appear content to spend their winter vacation right here where they were born. This mid-November afternoon boasts of perfect weather: a few high cirrus clouds, a light south wind, a high in the mid-sixties. House-sized boulders overlooking Styx Canyon at the west end of the refuge offer a view stretching out over a nearby farm with green winter wheat fields, the rectangular cropland surrounded by tall bottomland hardwoods including big oaks, walnuts and pecans.

My seat atop one of the boulders is excellent for wildlife watching both on the refuge and over the fence. Sprays of pale purple asters grow in creases amid the rock where dirt has collected, and a chestnut and white canyon wren bounces from boulder to boulder to keep me company. Soon four elk wander out of the timber and onto the distant wheat field and begin to graze. In time they're joined by a few turkeys, then more turkeys, then even more. I quit counting after reaching one hundred.

On my walk out of the wilderness area some 20 bison cross in front of me at a run, raising dust glowing like a huge halo in the evening light. A solitary bull, previously intent on grazing, hears the commotion, spots the movement, and quickly breaks into a sprint, doing his best to catch up to the galloping buffalo gals. There's no sign that anything in particular caused the animals to stampede; it was probably just a combination of good health and invigorating weather. A few minutes later, as the sun sinks behind a mountain, all is quiet except for the geese overhead. The buffalo probably have bedded down by now, but I can't stop thinking about how wild and free they looked as they bolted across the broad grassland, and what a spectacle it must have been to see six million all on the move at once, rather than today's six or sixteen or sixty.

Soon it will be Thanksgiving and seasonal change is once again in the air. The orange calves of spring are now the same dark brown as their mothers, gangly like two-legged teenagers and with body parts seemingly ill fit. It's difficult to believe that some of these ungainly young animals will grow into the majestic bulls that lord over these pastures. A few green leaves cling to some of the oaks and chittamwood trees, but for the most part the refuge has the barren, skeletal look of winter. A dark brown leopard frog catches autumn's waning rays from atop a rock in the middle of a creek flowing as clear as tap water. A flock of golden crowned kinglets, northerners arriving here to escape several months of snow, comb through the oaks, searching for tiny insect life. A ribbon snake, attractive in its red and yellow striped snakeskin suit, basks beside the stream beneath a hackberry tree peppered with tiny reddish fruit. Robins will descend on the hackberries later in the winter. But for now, a silver-gray northern harrier cruises just above the tops of wind-tossed grass, hoping to add protein to a meat-lover's diet in the form of any of that legion of May cottontail rabbit newborn that managed to survive a summer of serious predation.

The windy afternoon finds a dozen cow elk bedded in the pinkish little bluestem, while several bulls graze nearby. The rancor of the rut has been replaced by an urge to eat. The elk are in winter uniform: dark brown surrounding a pale tan to almost white saddle area, the cold weather coat featuring long guard hairs that catch the wind and whip around like the ponytail of a blonde riding in a convertible.

The weatherman says Thanksgiving will be cold, with a hard freeze the night before. That's good news for the deer hunters longing to wear some of their cold weather outfits, clothes that mostly take up space in the closet this far south. This year they'll be able to drag out synthetic down and insulated boots in preparation for a rendezvous with a swelling whitetail population that's responsible for hunter success ratios that would have seemed impossible 50 years ago. And, in a roundabout way, that's excellent news for Wichita Mountains buffalo. The U.S. Fish & Wildlife Service, responsible for running this place, draws revenue from fees paid by hunters and fishermen, plus special taxes on sporting goods including guns and ammunition.

Even at this late date the steep, north-facing walls of narrow canyons still have that New England look to them, with red leaves clinging to the refuge's scattered sugar maples and orange foliage on straight-trunked spotted oaks. It will all be gone following the upcoming hard freeze. But for now grasshoppers still sail 20 feet or more when I walk through swales of big bluestem. Gray-capped mushrooms grow from piles of buffalo dung and butterflies ride the wind while big, black, and shiny Bess beetles cross a dusty trail near my feet. Today the seasonal anthem consists of field sparrow song. Crows feeding on a fresh buffalo carcass keep quiet, having found an unexpected and much more nourishing outlet for their energies.

Late in the month the weather turns chilly, presaging what will be the norm in the weeks ahead. On this particular cool and foggy morning I've headed into the backcountry, camera in hand, hoping to photograph wildlife in some entrancing light.

Dense fog extends about halfway up the mountains, and the orange granite looks like fruit dipped in whipped cream. Elk grazing on a narrow saddle connecting a pair of low hills appear slightly yellow in the suffused light. A springfed stream pours over pink rock into a wooded bottom, where fog surrounds cottonwoods still wearing yellow leaves growing near a scattering of green elms. Flocks of titmice and juncos fly from tree to tree, searching for breakfast.

The valley where all the springs and creeks come together is broad and shallow, with enough deep soil to grow bountiful grass. As a consequence the old loner buffalo bulls like to sequester themselves here in the winter due to ample water, good grass, and shelter from the storms. And today, they're enjoying better than average scenery.

By mid-morning the bull occupying a particularly cozy portion of the valley *is* the scenery for anyone camera equipped. This old guy reminds me of some rugged tribal Scotsman in a Mel Gibson movie. The animal's topknot is thick, wild, and unruly, his body muscular and lean. Ribs are showing, but just faintly. The winter coat is thick and the color of Hershey's chocolate.

Even without the fog, this bull would be any artist's choice to grace at least one side of a nickel. Stir in the witchery of the moor-like background and the bull, a faint outline of an animal wrapped in a blue-gray veil, is pure and ghostly art.

Even more unnerving is the way this behemoth grazes in my direction, easing out of the fog and directly toward the boulder where I sit and snap pictures. When I lower the camera he's come within 15 feet and apparently plans to add my bootlaces to his breakfast. The appropriate thing to do is say adios and I do so without hesitation, merging with the fog and leaving the valley, and its most dominant resident, to the solitude both deserve.

Two days before the end of the month the first hard freeze turns shallow pools in the intermittent streams to ice. Winter is upon us, but apparently some of the so-called fragile species didn't get the memo. A bright red dragonfly circles on the wing as the sun climbs higher, the seemingly invincible insect circumnavigating a midday pool resembling a skating rink. Tomorrow's sunshine will turn ice to mud, and we've a little more than three weeks to prepare for whatever awaits beyond the winter solstice, a time when the sun seems little more than a decorative lantern too timid to turn away the agonizingly long nights.

SUNSET OVERLOOK. A December sun sets over the granite spine of the Wichitas, ancient landmark in the Southern Plains.

December

On the morning of the sixth of December the temperature is barely above freezing with wind blowing strongly from the south. The wind chill is such that walking in thick oak timber is more comfortable than walking across open prairie, especially oak timber on the north side of a tall ridge.

The ridge and trees block most of the wind, but the trail's a bit claustrophobic, considering the expansive views that prevail throughout much of the refuge. However it's chilly enough to forsake grandeur for comfort, and in this morning's case, for unexpected companionship. A shiny black Bess beetle, several inches long, is making tracks in the dust of a buffalo trail. Obviously a hardy insect, this particular beetle doesn't seem to care that we're sharing the trail only a few weeks prior to Christmas.

Bess beetles (Betsy bugs to many country people) are tough, interesting, and a bit of a conundrum among folks who look upon insects as something fit only for swatting, smashing, or drenching with chemicals. Bess beetles are highly social, forming pair bonds that include shared housecleaning duties. Both parents are excellent family beetles. They tend their wormlike larva, chewing up a pablum of wood mixed with beetle feces. The maturation process of larvae to beetle adult can take as long as 12 months, and the parents provide care throughout. They've been known to scoop Junior up in their stout mandibles and move to a safer sanctuary. Overall, Ma and Pa Bess beetle appear to meet the criteria of the region's often espoused family values.

Bess beetles head for the shelter of a rotting log when winter descends with a more virulent bite, but for now there's insect business to attend to here in the vicinity of the buffalo trail. Yet other than traffic here on the beetle interstate, there's not much happening on this chilly gray morning that portends more of the same. When the sun finally decides to shine about midday, a buffalo bull walks out of the oak grove windbreak and soon slumbers in the open, eager to soak up some winter rays. The massive animal is so relaxed that he doesn't even open his eyes when I amble past on my way back to the trailhead.

Six days later, the weather is 30 degrees warmer and sunny, yet with a strong north wind. It seems to be the sort of winter day that invigorates canyon wrens, or at least the one I've disturbed that keeps up a scolding chatter from a dead post oak tree.

A meadow between a pair of low ridges contains maybe a dozen bison cows that jump up when I approach and, rather than assume some defense posture or flee, decide to advance and get a closer look at Bigfoot. The cows follow for a while, then lose interest and wander away. Yet there's plenty of resident wildlife to watch: tiny midges gyrating over stream pools, each a speck of silver in the sunlight; grasshoppers with the body chemistry wherewithal to linger through the winter; sandhill cranes overhead, whinnying like mustang colts; flickers, this time the western or red-shafted variety, searching storm damaged oaks for insect infestation.

It's also a mid-December day featuring red dragonflies and yellow sulfur butterflies, the bright male dragonfly airborne in unity with its drab gray mate, the latter dipping her abdomen into a pool and leaving her progeny to the promise of spring. Bright green winter annual grasses already are growing taller in tight, damp canyons, and I'm sure the elk will visit at sundown, happy to have something succulent to balance the dry leaves and stems of grama grass. A snipe flushes from a damp meadow tucked between massive folds of pink granite. A tiny stream, not more than a couple of feet wide at its widest point, trickles through the middle of dark earth that promises earthworms. My guess is that the snipe will be back for more earthworm probing as soon as I'm out of sight.

On the way out of the wilderness area the late evening sunlight frames a beautiful buffalo bull, an extremely dark animal with a head that's almost blue-black. The bull rolls in a buffalo wallow, rises to shake off a cloud of dust, then breaks into a run. After a sprint of about one hundred yards, the bull skids to a stop like a well-trained quarter horse, drops down to roll in another wallow, pops back up, shakes, then starts out again at a run, stopping at a closely cropped patch of green grass. The bull's gears switch from overdrive to neutral, and just as suddenly he's a placid animal again, grazing calmly for as long as I care to stand here and watch.

The impulses that drive buffalo can change a calm bull into an animal with the raging strength to toss a horse skyward. Visitors here who mistakenly assume that these seemingly slow, unfeeling brutes are stupid and tame do so at their own peril. I've seen bulls charge photographers who've crept too close, while other visitors have learned the hard way that a drunken idea for a portrait taken with a 2,000-pound bison can land you in a tree. Over the years I've found that when that spindly little tail goes straight up, bison anger is about to erupt. Best to give the animals wide berth no matter the season or sexes. They're easy enough to observe and photograph from a safe distance, and after all it's their refuge.

Sundown illuminates backlit seeds on pink-tinted little bluestem grass, each seed glowing with the sheen of polished chrome. It's a beautiful late evening sun that shines here in December, the dazzling light a perfect curtain call for several hours spent in introspection earlier in the afternoon, amid a dark oak grove deep in the wilderness. The refuge harbors scattered ancient groves featuring trees with trunks as big around as 55 gallon drums, perfect for waiting out a snowstorm or popping the clutch on an imagination prone to slipping into overdrive.

Sitting quietly in a Wichita Mountains version of a Druid forest generally produces watchable wildlife, and this oak grove sit-in was no exception. A whitetail buck came around a chunk of vertical granite just in time to nearly collide with a buffalo bull coming from the opposite direction. They froze, nearly nose to nose, and I fought to keep from laughing at what were truly looks of amazement on two chiseled animal faces.

Then, just a day later, a sunny afternoon featuring a balmy south wind and a high in the low seventies flipped into the deep freeze when the weather gods tossed a switch. A covey of bobwhite quail searched for brushy cover at the edge of an oak grove as the wind switched, blowing from the north, and the temperature dropped like a fishing sinker in Lake Lawtonka. Even the geese overhead, returning to the refuge after visiting nearby winter wheat fields, seemed to be talking about the abrupt change. By the next morning it was winter again in the Wichitas, with temperatures in the teens and a wind that felt like an icy scalpel.

December means that soon it will be Christmas in Medicine Park, the little town on the banks of Medicine Creek at the refuge's east entrance. Medicine Park advertises itself as a "cobblestone community" because of the unique stone incorporated into most of the early buildings. The rock of choice was a naturally occurring, rounded orange granite about the size of bowling or basketballs, gathered from throughout the mountains.

Medicine Park, with its hobbit-like aura, has been a popular place to visit since early in the 1900s, when it gained fame as a resort community. At its height this strange little town boasted of resort hotels, quaint cabins, swimming in the stone basin pools of Medicine Creek, country-style dining, and ample illegal drinking during the Prohibition era.

Bootleggers made sure that visitors to Medicine Park had access to spirits, and the resort became a hideaway for those a step ahead of the law. One modern cabin claims to have housed Texas outlaws Bonnie and Clyde, and a local once told me that another was a favored refuge for mobster Al Capone. The resort grew from a big tent serving hot meals next to the swimming hole into a resort luring north Texans with two inns, a spa, dance hall, canteen, petting zoo, general store, bath house, and bait shop. The swimming area was landscaped and featured foot bridges and areas for sunbathing. The resort flourished from the late teens to the 1930s, providing a getaway where both the rich and famous and the notorious could mingle and relax. Visitors included actor/newspaper columnist Will Rogers, aviator Wiley Post, Frank Phillips of Phillips Petroleum, country music innovator Bob Wills, cowboy actors Roy Rogers and Dale Evans, and Oklahoma's very own robber of renown, Pretty Boy Floyd.

The Great Depression of the 1930s brought an end to the boisterous times that flourished during Medicine Park's original lifespan. Over time the little town grew rundown and most of the businesses closed. By the late sixties about all that remained were a tavern, a private club, and the dining room in the Old Plantation Hotel, where patrons could walk in the front door and see their soon-to-be meal swimming in a horse trough. The hotel kept live catfish, one of their more favored entrees, stocked, fresh and close at hand.

By the early 1970s, Medicine Park mostly consisted of a few locals who'd lived here all their lives, soldiers who'd hung around when their enlistment was up at Fort Sill, counter-culture types drawn to the community's weirdness and weekenders in search of a good hamburger served in the shadow of Mount Scott. I can recall summer weekends when the pools below the waterfalls in the Forty Foot Hole area of Cache Creek swarmed with skinny dippers, a crowd with a fondness for the era's herb of choice. In Medicine Park a Fort Sill dropout would, on weekend evenings, don a long black monk's robe with a hood, grab a death's head-adorned walking staff and prowl the streets, each step seemingly carrying him higher than Elk Mountain. Good musicians hung out here, and young people alienated from society seemed to feel at home in this once fashionable resort that mainstream America had chosen to dismiss.

Then even the Medicine Park mainstays, the Riverside Café and the Old Plantation Restaurant, closed their doors. By the 1980s federal officials were taking measures to clean up the two-legged wildlife hanging out at the refuge in an effort to restore its original mission: a place for nature, rather than party central. It seemed that the little community at the east gate had finally breathed its last bohemian gasp. But the stream flowing through the middle of town had a reputation for healing, and heal it did.

In the mid-1990s a new generation grew intrigued with Medicine Park's unique history, and began to buy into the town itself. In time the unconventional community with a population of less than a thousand watched as renovation and restoration jumpstarted a transfusion that, at the time of this writing, had resulted in 50 new businesses, a winery, a bed and breakfast, cabins, gift shops, and good dining at the resurrected Riverside and Old Plantation restaurants. Medicine Creek's been cleaned up, the swimming area reopened and a new pedestrian bridge put in place. The town claims an inordinate number of sculptors, fine artists, designers, actors, and musicians, and new homes dot the granite slopes overlooking the little hamlet. Even so, there's not a lot of polish to this place that seems to have more lives than the feral cats roaming the alleyways. It's been put back together with ample buffalo country funkiness left in place in just the right amounts. In many ways Medicine Park has become a living tribute to what a few bison, given a home of their own, has meant to an area that otherwise would be just another army town among the many sprinkled throughout the Southern Plains.

Late in the month it's grown warm again and I'm beyond the refuge fences, visiting the headwaters of Medicine Creek with a local landowner. The stream sounds like some counterpart from the Smokies this afternoon as it splashes over riffles and settles into deep green pools. Like all the streams born in the uplifted rock north of the refuge, Medicine Creek at this point in its journey is hauntingly beautiful when rains have been kind. The terrain merges a gallery forest of post and spotted oaks with ridges of familiar orange granite. The streambed is smooth, bluish rock studded with big, blue-gray boulders, and springs scattered throughout the area feed the current with rivulets running clear and cold.

Rocks plucked from the current reveal a menagerie of aquatic insect larvae similar to what you'd expect from an Ozark stream hundreds of miles to the east. Well oxygenated riffles produce mayfly nymphs, caddis larvae, and tiny cases constructed of granite grit that protect these same brown and green caddis "worms," bugs well known to trout fishermen in higher country and colder waters.

Here, however, the piscatorial quarry is largemouth bass, living in the habitat the fish evolved in, healthy and fat, a stream fish long before the first reservoir or farm pond came into the picture.

The landowner is an excellent angler, and while I examine clear, snotty gel beneath a rock and recognize it as the stream's future snail population, he's catching bass averaging around two pounds apiece, strong fish with vivid green, black, and white markings. Winter midges are dancing over Medicine Creek by the time we're ready to leave that afternoon, and the rumble of the stream serves as background music for the high-pitched keen of wood ducks flushed from one of the longer pools. Cricket frogs leap from the bank and into the stream, each performing the typical cricket frog maneuver of swimming a few strokes and then abruptly turning back towards the bank to become motionless at the edge of the water.

During the walk back to the truck the landowner tells of booty discovered by his wife when she's combed this part of the stream in search of stone artifacts. Her collection, presented proudly when we return to their home, includes flint or chert scrapers, drills, and projectile points of several shapes and sizes. It seems that the beauty and natural utility of the place have appealed to visitors for thousands of years.

As the end of the month draws near, another of the refuge's schizophrenic weather moods results in thundershowers more reminiscent of May. In the storm's aftermath, sunny skies and a strong southwest wind reveal a bright, warm landscape with an afternoon high in the upper fifties and countless buffalo wallows filled with water. Temporary waterfalls bounce from cliffs and boulders, and by late afternoon the sun shines like a spotlight on rock the color of orange sherbet and wallows that reflect like mirrors. At sunset dozens of deer come out to browse in the big prairie near the east gate. It's a tranquil scene that's beautiful beyond reckoning, but I can't help thinking that it's only a short time until the weather catches up with the calendar, and the job of survival begins.

The week prior to Christmas is perfect for area retailers pushing winter woolens, hats and gloves, but ominous for wildlife. The highest temperature reading strains to break forty, and the Wichitas receive light yet repeated dustings of snow and freezing rain. A walk along an intermittent stream now standing in icy pools reveals first the nervous clucking of a flock of turkeys, then their long, downhill flight into thick timber. Later I spot a small bird huddled up on a limb reaching out over a deep pool and realize that it's an eastern phoebe, a flycatcher you'd think would be somewhere much farther south by now, a place more tropical and blessed by ample bugs. But obviously the amount of insect life on the winter refuge is deceiving—the ongoing midge hatch seems to be enough to supply needed calories, and this comely little bird fond of making quick dashes from a low branch to secure its meals would rather face the cold than flee the country.

But even a phoebe tends to reconsider when a blizzard arrives on sixty-mile-per-hour winds. And that's what happens on Christmas Eve. The storm drops anywhere from seven to 14 inches of snow over the area, which the wind promptly stacks into four to five feet drifts. Winter storms of such magnitude don't happen very often here, and for several days the normal bustle of Christmas is held at a standstill. But by the 28th the sun is out, the south wind a balmy omen and melting begins in earnest.

I receive my surprise Christmas present when a walk into the wilderness reveals a mature golden eagle, solemn in shades of rich brown and burnished gold, perched in what remains of the upper limbs of a long dead mesquite tree. A flock of 50 or more wild turkeys are scratching and pecking away at whatever they can uncover in the way of food along the snow-rimmed banks of Medicine Creek. And a seasonal influx of mountain bluebirds has arrived, maybe from Colorado or New Mexico, birds matching the color of the sunlit sky when flushed from thick shelter of eastern red cedars.

But it's the buffalo that show how evolution has prepared the species for such weather. Solitary bulls shove the snow aside with massive heads, searching for the dried grass that will feed them for several months. Dark buffalo cows and calves move from deep snow to where the fierce winds have swept the drifts from low ridges, uncovering the bland brown sprigs of blue grama.

One of the cows moves more slowly than the rest, and as she approaches I see the long and gaping wound in the folds of skin under her front foreleg. The wound is festering and oozes green pus. It appears that this cow has clashed with a dominant matriarch, and been hooked with a sharp, curved horn for her troubles. She'll battle both winter storms and infection for as long as her health and willpower hold out. After that, flowers will grow through her bleached white bones when April returns, and coyotes will dream dreams of a mid-winter smorgasbord—a belated Christmas gift fit for the clever, cunning and always hungry song dog.

Conclusion: A Last, Great Place

A spring day, cool and party cloudy. A morning in the mid-forties that's morphed into the seventies by mid-afternoon. Rain fell the week before, and the Wichita Mountains grass is green, flowers bright red, blue, and yellow, buffalo calves a playful reddish orange, prairie dog pups the color of pale sand and as frisky as little terriers. A perfect day, basically, to be in one of the nation's oldest managed wildlife refuges, and visitors have descended in droves.

The parking lot is full at the prairie dog town bordering the main east–west road through the refuge. A camera club from Oklahoma City, represented by maybe a dozen members, stalks the lively little rodents, tripods poised like shotguns in the hands of trap shooters. The prairie dogs are cooperating mainly by their sheer fecundity. New pups seem everywhere. One burrow holds three, heads out, scanning the crowd. Others either wrestle with littermates or cling tightly to their mothers. It looks like a good year, population-wise, for the prairie dog colony, but members of the photo club are worried. "Where are the mothers," one concerned woman asks a fellow photographer. "All I'm seeing are little pups."

CACHE CREEK FALLS. Cache Creek drops over stair-stepping waterfalls in the Forty Foot Hole portion of the refuge.

The man pauses for a moment, obviously thoughtful although clueless, then ad libs his reply. "Well, the refuge has to kill them. Culling the herd, you know."

Another photographer standing nearby chimes in. "I think it's all the hawks and eagles," she says with the wisdom of a four-year-old seeking to impress a playmate. "The birds only eat the adults because, if they're going to the trouble to eat prairie dogs, they want the biggest meal."

I start to explain about prairie dog population dynamics, litter size, predation, and such, then realize that facts aren't nearly as much fun as making up some wildly concocted story. So, while the nice folks with their cameras banter biologically bereft prairie dog theories back and forth, I wander in search of buffalo.

As usual, I didn't have to wander far. Buffalo gravitate to prairie dog towns. Maybe a dozen cows were resting at the edge of the dog town, accompanied by about a half dozen very small and very orange newborn calves, each youngster stretched out in the sun, soaking up some rays.

Buffalo cows aren't too tolerant of upright two-leggeds who advance upon their newborn, so it's best to photograph the youngsters with a telephoto lens. It's a fact of life too often ignored by camera-toting tourists, who press forward at their own peril. The quest for the perfect snapshot is the bane of wildlife refuges from Yosemite to Yellowstone—people mistake familiarity for tameness and push past an invisible boundary that, once crossed, propels protective mothers into battle mode.

Not far from the prairie dog town, nine elk huddle in a tight group in the middle of a large prairie. Pacing nervously, they wait until automobile traffic clears so they can continue their march to Elk Mountain in safety. The animals, winter coats partially shed, look especially ragged, the wind tossing remaining long hairs that contrast the short, neat sheen of the felt-like summer wardrobe.

All of the bull elk have shed their antlers except for one, a young animal with a pair of simple appendages approximately two feet long without forks or branches, the type of antlers commonly referred to as spikes. In a few years he'll wear a massive rack with maybe a half dozen prongs on each side, headgear that will prove to be a heavy crown and an invitation to battle. But for now the young male is just a spike, a boy with pimples, a target for aggression from the big guys and disdain from the ladies. The long guard hairs on the creature's neck stand straight out in the spring wind, and he looks more like something native to Africa. No wonder he's clung to his antlers for as long as he can—maybe they offer some solace in an adolescent world where respect is limited.

In a few minutes the coast is clear and the cows, yearlings, and bulls with nubs where antlers once were hurry across the highway and into the timber bordering Elk Mountain. A tom turkey with a long beard whipping in the wind follows, although it appears his journey has more to do with a hen that's already crossed and entered the timber—after all, it *is* spring. There's a little time to kill while I wait for the buffalo calves to rise and present themselves to be photographed, so I study the new fiddleheads about to unfurl on a wooly lip fern, the foliage silvery green and extremely hairy, a plant seemingly out of place amid a jumble of granite boulders and cactus.

Rocky, barren aspects of the refuge tend to fool those who focus on the piles of granite and fail to remember that this is the life zone where east meets west. Most of the trainees from nearby Fort Sill that I've talked to, especially those from the east coast, refer to the surrounding terrain as desert. And that's probably what it seems to them after a long and dusty day on artillery maneuvers.

They don't realize that the refuge contains enough cool microhabitats to support sugar maples, and that ringtail cats more common to the true desert Southwest are seen on occasion. Such variety is rare among our public lands, and the refuge provides an excellent outdoor laboratory for ecologists studying niche habitats and the progression of climate from wet to dry following the last ice age. Grassland ecologists have the opportunity to see samples of the Southern Plains in a near natural state, considering that the refuge has been grazed by buffalo rather than commercial livestock for over a century. And, for the poet or romantic, the Wichitas remain a place to prowl with the ghosts of a rich western history: Custer, Sheridan, Sherman, Quanah, Satanta, Satank. They all put down tracks in these mountains.

Ever since its inception, passionate people have wanted this refuge to be something it is not. Miners, until they were driven away from the rocks by the army, wanted the Wichitas to be the next big gold strike. Early boosters wanted a national park. Later, as nearby Lawton grew and the refuge became an increasingly popular tourist attraction and playground, individuals including newspaper editors and chamber of commerce boosters wanted less emphasis on wildlife and more on the creation of a great theme park that would generate revenue for nearby communities. Some boosters wanted horseback riding trails back in the North Mountain area; others wanted more roads in, and all fences out. Few wanted anything as plain and simple as a federal wildlife refuge. Eventually the refuge began to offer guided educational tours into some of the restricted areas. But, by and large, the refuge remains largely managed for the well-being of wildlife. The staff's common sense efforts to keep the area as natural as possible with people restricted to a public use area has never been enough for those who see the Wichitas as a park for people rather than a refuge for species that were once nearly extinct.

Over the years refuge personnel have done a number of things within their budgetary power to make the refuge a unique educational experience and keep wildlife viewing compatible with an increasing number of visitors. Since the early 1970s the majority of these visitors have demonstrated an increasing desire for natural, wildlife-related experiences in a world increasingly dominated by computers, cell phones, and games on a flashing screen. Nostalgia also has played a part in the refuge's popularity. Few things reflect the spirit of the old, wild West more than a herd of buffalo grazing in a natural setting. Geronimo's grave is just a few miles away in the Apache cemetery at Fort Sill. And George Armstrong Custer wrote a book about his Indian chasing time here, a book in which this great American hero reveals a rather average brain completely overwhelmed with arrogance and bravado.

In a better world this refuge would be much, much bigger, capable of hosting a thundering herd of thousands rather than a few hundred buffalo. Additional acres would allow it to more truthfully replicate the awesome sweep of wild horizon witnessed and noted by cowboys and cavalry officers who climbed to the mountaintops to take it all in. Unfortunately an extended Fort Sill borders the refuge to the south, while Lake Lawtonka and the swelling community of Medicine Park occupy the eastern boundary. This leaves expansion opportunities to the west and north only, mostly big ranches that real estate developers would covet should they ever come up for sale.

As the area's popularity continues to grow, some fear that the refuge won't be able to handle the projected amount of visitor traffic foreseen for the near future, much less 50 years from now. Already environmentalists are calling attention to a growing problem with industrial haze, and it's doubtful that the federal wildlife refuge system, with its limited budget, can afford to fix all the ills of an area that finds itself increasingly loved to death.

Maybe the boosters of the early 1900s were right—the Wichitas should have achieved national park status, along with enough acreage to make the park a viable one. At about the same time, folks in the Texas Panhandle lobbied for national park status for Palo Duro Canyon near Amarillo, a spectacular hole in the earth second in size only to the Grand Canyon in Arizona. But, as with the Wichitas, lawmakers declined to press the case, and the Southern Plains had to be content with scattered state parks and limited public land.

A better fit for the Wichitas or Palo Duro might have been national monument status, lands set aside to celebrate the Southern Plains Indian culture largely ignored after the reservations were disbanded and the tribes assimilated into local towns and cities. Oklahoma, like her sister state to the south, adheres to a conservative philosophy that every acre of God's green earth should be privately owned and fiscally productive. Still, ranchland bordering the refuge to the west and northwest contains a large amount of native grass grazing land with beautiful granite outcrops, springs, and streams, important historical sites and landmarks that have spiritual meaning within Kiowa and Comanche cultures. If these borderlands might someday be acquired, over time, from willing sellers, the refuge could grow to include entire watersheds, tracts of mesquite grassland, and eventually enough room for a buffalo herd that would physically represent this unique landscape as it existed prior to white encroachment—the "buffalo commons" concept that people in the region disdain but which could be the final answer for a landscape prone to be rendered agriculturally impractical by reoccurring drought.

That's the dream of some of us who want a living natural history textbook dedicated to the Old West, an open air memorial to cowboys and Indians and buffalo on an appropriately big scale. Such a dream would need a charismatic champion, but such an individual would be aided by the fact that a Southern Plains "buffalo commons" is increasingly an idea whose time has come.

In many ways the Wichita Mountains have become a national attraction by demand if not by design, drawing well over a million visitors annually from throughout the United States. An enlarged refuge would be an economic boon to a local area that would desperately need one if or when several nearby military bases are drawn down and an already shrinking oil economy eventually plays out. Also, if predictions for more and prolonged droughts due to climate change have any merit, the region's wheat farmers will be forced to walk away from land that has supported some form of agriculture for more than a century. At that time, most farmland will be converted back to grassland, as it was during the Dust Bowl drought of the 1930s when private land was absorbed by the federal government and became today's national grasslands.

Area farmers and ranchers got a sampling of what climate change might mean to their traditional way of life in 2010 to 2011, when rain ceased to fall in October of 2010 and did not return for nearly a year.

By the spring of 2011 people in Oklahoma and Texas were beginning to understand that this weather aberration was exceptional. Spring rains failed to materialize, and parched pastures either stayed brown, or became that way as sunburnt and water-starved plants returned to dormancy. With no cooling rains to moderate soil temperatures, daily high temperatures quickly climbed over 100 degrees and remained there through the summer. It was the hottest, driest period ever recorded in much of Texas and Oklahoma, and everything suffered: plants, animals, birds, the people who depend upon farm crops or cattle grazing for their income.

Much of the wheat harvest failed, and ranchers were forced to liquidate their herds. By midsummer they were out of both grass and water—ponds and creeks had gone dry. Hay was at a premium, and shipped in from sources hundreds of miles away. Soon even imported hay grew scarce.

Ranchers whose families had been on the land for generations were out of business, with little hope of ever getting back in. And, when it seemed that the weather couldn't get any worse, the fires came.

In late June artillery training on Fort Sill touched off a fire that quickly spread to the north, threatening the community of Medicine Park. Heat, drought, and 30 mile-per-hour winds kept the fire unmanageable, and quickly led to the evacuation of some 500 homes. Of the 1,500 residents evacuated, 13 families found they had no homes to return to when the 5,500-acre blaze was finally contained at the edge of the resort community.

Firefighters fought the Medicine Park fire in temperatures that approached 110 degrees. Three months later daily highs were still pushing the century mark, the drought was still in place and another fatal spark resulted in a fire that consumed approximately one-half of the wildlife refuge as well as private land bordering it on the north and northwest.

The refuge fire spread into impassable areas and continued to burn for five days, killing mature trees, destroying 11 homes outside the refuge and charring numerous barns and outbuildings. By the time the fire burned itself out the refuge was a charred mess, a grim stage of destruction that reminded me of Yellowstone following the fire of 1988.

Refuge officials moved the longhorn herd to grazing lands on Fort Sill, reassured the public that they'd keep the buffalo in good health by supplemental feeding if necessary and pointed out that much of the trees and brush torched by the flames were there due to years of fire suppression. As one refuge worker admitted, the staff had differing opinions on what the resulting plant communities would look like the following spring if rains returned to nurture them. However most agreed that the reduction of forest, especially invasive eastern red cedar, would leave the refuge a lot more like it used to be prior to settlement.

Rainfall did return in the spring of 2012, and blackened areas greened up rapidly and early. By the end of May the wildflower display was stunning, and the variety of species as diverse as I've ever seen it. Buffalo bulls lounging around the prairie dog towns were butter fat and in excellent condition for the upcoming breeding season. The most noticeable difference was the acreage of charred oak brush, and the blackened trunks of tall post oaks that no longer blocked sunlight from a robust ground cover of grass and colorful forbs.

In a way it seemed that the Wichitas had been to hell and back. Blackened woodlands were replaced by vast fields of flowers and the butterflies that helped pollinate them. Biologists absorbed the hows and whys of fire ecology from a textbook spread open under the sky. Science could scrutinize the landscape and see both catastrophe and resurrection. The refuge was doing its job. It has absorbed a decimating blow from the worst extremes of Southern Plains weather, and now it was bouncing back.

But then, that's why visionary men wanted to protect places like this in the first place. Refuges are, as pioneer ecologist Aldo Leopold pointed out, lands set aside to retain all of the biological working parts. Or, as someone once put it, the green blueprints for God's master plan. Then, when mankind's activities result in some sort of natural crisis, we're left with benchmarks, natural laboratories functioning somewhat close to the original, biotic information to tinker with and hopefully help restore the order that results in generational health.

At the same time, John Q. Public has an opportunity to walk among buffalo, elk, prairie dogs, and deer, much in the manner of men like Kicking Bird and Quanah Parker. It's not quite a ticket for a ride in a time machine. But considering how far we've drifted away from the original Eden, and the destruction we've left in our wake as we drifted, it's still getting pretty darned close.

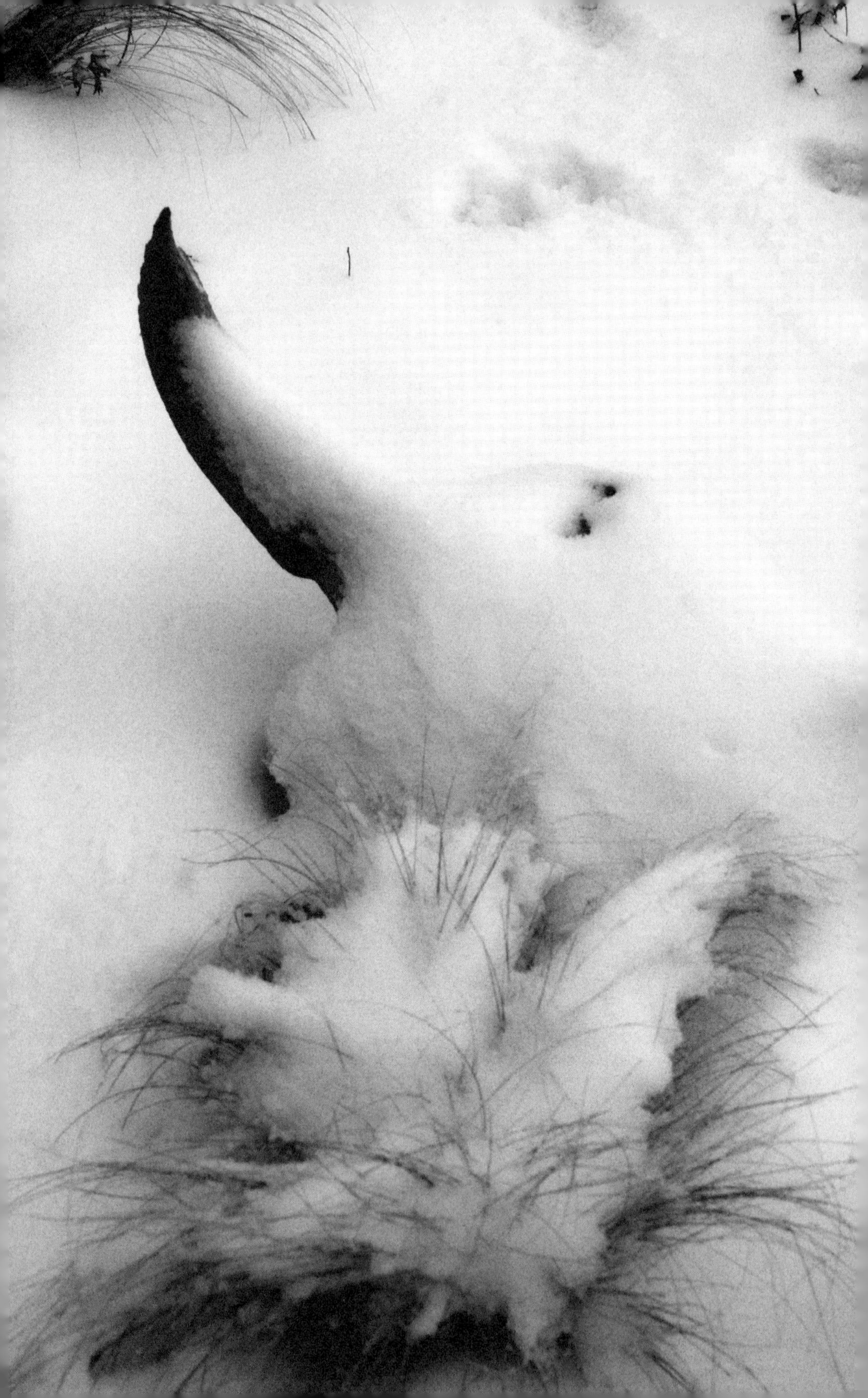

GONE BUT NOT FORGOTTEN. A bleached buffalo skull blends with new snow blanketing refuge grasslands.

Bibliography

HISTORY

Battey, Thomas C. *The Life and Adventures of a Quaker Among the Indians*. Norman: University of Oklahoma Press, 1968.

Cook, John. *The Border and the Buffalo*. 1907. Repr., Austin: State House Press, 1967.

DeSpain, S. Matthew. "For Society's Sake: The Wichita Mountains, Wildlife, and Identity in Oklahoma's Early Environmental History." *The Chronicles of Oklahoma* 78, no. 4 (2000): 388–411.

Ellenbrook, Edward Charles. *Outdoor and Trail Guide to the Wichita Mountains of Southwest Oklahoma*. Lawton, OK: In the Valley of the Wichitas House, 1983.

Halloran, Art. *The Nature Man's Stories of the Wichita Mountains*. Lawton, OK: Lawton Constitution, 1972.

Jordan, Julia. *Plains Apache Ethnobotany*. Norman: University of Oklahoma Press, 2008.

Lehmann, Herman. *Nine Years Among the Indians*. Albuquerque: University of New Mexico Press, 1993.

Momaday, N. Scott. *The Way to Rainy Mountain*. Albuquerque: University of New Mexico Press, 1969.

Neeley, Bill. *The Last Comanche Chief: The Life and Times of Quanah Parker*. New York: John Wiley & Sons, 1997.

Nye, Wilbur Sturdevant. *Bad Medicine and Good: Tales of the Kiowas*. Norman: University of Oklahoma Press, 1962.

———. *Carbine and Lance: The Story of Old Fort Sill*. Norman: University of Oklahoma Press, 1937.

Wallace, Ernest, and E. Adamson Hoebel. *The Comanches: Lords of the South Plains*. Norman: University of Oklahoma Press, 1952.

William C. Meadows. *Kiowa Ethnogeography*. Austin: University of Texas Press, 2008.

NATURAL HISTORY

Abbott, John C. *Dragonflies and Damselflies of Texas and the South-Central United States*. Princeton, NJ: Princeton University Press, 2005.

Ajilvsgi, Geyata. *Wildflowers of Texas*. Bryan, TX: Shearer Publishing, 1984.

Bare, Janel E. *Wildflowers and Weeds of Kansas*. Lawrence: University Press of Kansas, 1979.

Bert, William H., and Richard P. Grossenheider. *A Field Guide to the Mammals of America North of Mexico*. Boston: Houghton Mifflin, 1976.

Burill, Larry C., Steven A. Dewey, David W. Cudney, B. E. Nelson. *Weeds of the West*. Edited by Tom D. Whitson. 5th ed. Np: The Western Society of Weed Science, 1996.

Caire, William, Jack D. Tyler, Bryan P. Glass, and Michael A. Mares. *Mammals of Oklahoma*. Norman: University of Oklahoma Press, 1989.

Clark, William S., and Brian K. Wheeler. *Hawks*. Boston: Houghton Mifflin, 1987.

Cobb, Boughton. *Ferns*. Boston: Houghton Mifflin, 1984.

Collins, Scott L., and Linda L. Wallace, eds. *Fire in North American Tallgrass Prairies*. Norman: University of Oklahoma Press, 1990.

Conant, Roger. *Field Guild to Reptiles and Amphibians of Eastern and Central North America*. 1958. Repr., Boston: Houghton Mifflin, 1975.

Curson, Jon, David Quinn, and David Beadle. *Warblers of the Americas*. Boston: Houghton Mifflin, 1994.

Dary, David A. *The Buffalo Book*. Chicago: Swallow Press, 1974.

Davis, Linda W. *Weed Seeds of the Great Plains*. Lawrence: University Press of Kansas, 1993.

Degenhardt, William G., Charles W. Painter, and Andrew H. Price. *Amphibians and Reptiles of New Mexico*. Albuquerque: University of New Mexico Press, 1996.

Dethier, Vincent G. *Crickets and Katydids: Concerts and Solos*. Cambridge, MA: Harvard University Press, 1992.

Dole, John M., Walter P. Gerard, and John M. Nelson. *Butterflies of Oklahoma, Kansas, and North Texas*. Norman: University of Oklahoma Press, 2004.

Eaton, Eric R., and Kenn Kaufman. *Kaufman Field Guide to Insects of North America*. Boston: Houghton Mifflin, 2007.

Emerton, James H. *The Common Spiders of the United States*. New York: Dover Publications, 1961.

Freeman, Craig C., and Eileen K. Schofield. *Roadside Wildflowers of the Southern Great Plains*. Lawrence: University Press of Kansas, 1991.

Gard, Wayne. *The Great Buffalo Hunt*. Lincoln: University of Nebraska Press, 1968.

Gould, Frank W. *Common Texas Grasses: An Illustrated Guide*. College Station: Texas A&M University Press, 1978.

———. *Grasses of the Southwestern United States*. Tucson: University of Arizona Press, 1951.

Great Plains Flora Association. *Flora of the Great Plains*. Lawrence: University Press of Kansas, 1986.

Guthery, Fred S. *On Bobwhites*. College Station: Texas A&M University Press, 2000.

Haines, Francis. *The Buffalo*. New York: Thomas Y. Crowell Company, 1970.

Hatch, Stephan L., and Jennifer Pluhar. *Texas Range Plants*. College Station: Texas A&M University Press, 1993.

Heitzman, J. Richard, and Joan E. Heitzman. *Butterflies and Moths of Missouri*. Np: Missouri Department of Conservation, 1987.

Hoogland, John L. *The Black-Tailed Prairie Dog: Social Life of a Burrowing Mammal*. Chicago: University of Chicago Press, 1995.

———., ed. *Conservation of the Black-Tailed Prairie Dog: Saving North America's Western Grasslands*. Washington, D.C.: Island Press, 2006.

Hornaday, William Temple. *The Extermination of the American Bison*. 1889. Repr., Washington, D.C.: Smithsonian Institution Press, 2002.

Isenberg, Andrew C. *The Destruction of the Bison: An Environmental History, 1750–1920*. New York: Cambridge University Press, 2000.

Johnsgard, Paul A. *Great Wildlife of the Great Plains*. Lawrence: University Press of Kansas, 2003.

———. *Prairie Birds: Fragile Splendor in the Great Plains*. Lawrence: University Press of Kansas, 2001.

———. *Prairie Dog Empire: A Saga of the Shortgrass Prairie*. Lincoln: University of Nebraska Press, 2005.

Kindscher, Kelly. *Edible Wild Plants of the Prairie*. Lawrence: University Press of Kansas, 1987.

———. *Medicinal Wild Plants of the Prairie*. Lawrence: University Press of Kansas, 1992.

Kirkpatrick, Zoe Merriman. *Wildflowers of the Western Plains*. Austin: University of Texas Press, 1992.

Ladd, Doug. *Tallgrass Prairie Wildflowers*. Helena, MT: Falcon Press, 1995.

Lott, Dale F. *American Bison: A Natural History*. Berkeley: University of California Press, 2002.

Martin, Alexander C., Herbert S. Zim, and Arnold L. Nelson. *American Wildlife and Plants: A Guide to Wildlife Food Habits*. New York: Dover Publications, 1951.

McCoy, Doyle. *Roadside Flowers of Oklahoma*. Np: C & J Printing Company, 1976.

McHugh, Tom. *Time of the Buffalo*. 1972. Repr., Lincoln: University of Nebraska Press, 1979.

Miller, Rudolph J., and Henry W. Robison. *The Fishes of Oklahoma*. Stillwater: Oklahoma State University Press, 1973.

Murdy, William H., and M. Eloise Browncarter. *Guide to the Plants of Granite Outcrops*. Athens: University of Georgia Press, 2000.

Murie, Olaus J. *Field Guide to Animal Tracks*. Boston: Houghton Mifflin, 1975.

Pasture and Range Plants. Bartlesville, OK: Phillips Petroleum Company, 1963.

Paulson, Dennis. *Dragonflies and Damselflies of the West*. Princeton: Princeton University Press, 2009.

Pennak, Robert W. *Fresh-water Invertebrates of the United States*. 2nd ed. Hoboken, NJ: John Wiley & Sons, 1978.

Range Plant Handbook. 1937. Repr., New York: Dover Publications, 1988.

Rising, James D. *A Guide to the Identification and Natural History of the Sparrows of the United States and Canada*. New York: Academic Press, 1996.

Sibley, David Allen. *Sibley Guide to Birds*. New York: Knopf, 2000.

Sutton, George Miksch. *Oklahoma Birds*. Norman: University of Oklahoma Press, 1974.

Thomas, Jack Ward, and Dale E. Toweill, eds. *Elk of North America: Ecology and Management*. Harrisburg, PA: Stackpole Books, 1982.

Trelease, William. *Winter Botany*. 1931. Repr., New York: Dover Publications, 1967.

Tyrel, Ronald J., Terrence G. Bidwell, and Ronald E. Masters. *Field Guide to Oklahoma Plants*. Stillwater: Oklahoma State University, 2002.

Vines, Robert A. *Trees of North Texas*. Austin: University of Texas Press, 1982.

Weaver, J. E. *Native Vegetation of Nebraska*. Lincoln: University of Nebraska Press, 1965.

———. *Prairie Plants and their Environment*. Lincoln: University of Nebraska Press, 1968.

Weniger, Del. *Cacti of Texas and Neighboring States*. Austin: University of Texas Press, 1984.

White, Richard E. *Beetles*. Boston: Houghton Mifflin, 1998.

GEOLOGY

Johnson, Kenneth S. *Geologic History of Oklahoma*. Oklahoma Geological Society, Educational Publication 9:2008, University of Oklahoma, Norman.

Weisburd, Stefi. *A Fault of Youth* (Meers Fault). Accessed on ScienceNews.org

Index

Page numbers in *italics* indicate illustrations.